SHOES Without Feet

SHOES Without Feet: A Journey of Strength, Hope, Overcoming Obstacles, Encouragement & Success

Dr. Chantrise Sims Holliman

Published by Disturb the Universe, LLC

SHOES WITHOUT FEET

Published by Disturb the Universe, LLC

Printed in the United States of America

ISBN-13: 978-0-9986219-1-3

And for These I Give Thanks

Over the past year and a half, I have learned the meaning of love. This is not to say that I didn't know it before, but if you really want to know who's in your corner, go through a traumatic experience and see who's still there standing with you, and in some cases, holding you up.

Insert Shout of Praise Here

To Mom and Dad: Thank you for being my forever cheerleaders, my rocks, the people who raised me to face my challenges head on. **Mom**, thanks for spending the first almost year of your retirement taking care or me and making sure every "I" was dotted, and every "t" was crossed. Every nurse and every doctor in every hospital knew you by name and wanted no part of being on the other side of your wrath. Thank you for not killing me when you were on the receiving end of my attitudinal rants and for being my "plus one" when I dove back into presenting at the ASCD conference. Vacation next year is on me! I think…**Dad,** you've been my biggest fan since I read *Danny the Dinosaur* to you on the sofa when I was two. You always know what to say and how to say and when to say. You also know when not to say anything at all. You believe in me when I don't even believe in me and I will forever be your girl. I love you both.

To Astede: We both know that you are my "Mini Me" because we look alike, but you're also my "Mini Me" because we talk alike and think alike. One of the things I love most about you is your ability to throw my advice back at me when I need it most. It's also one of the most frustrating. Who told you to remember everything I ever told you? Geesh. Your strength over this past year blows my mind and your belief in me got me through many a day and night. I love you Doodle. You make me so proud to be your mom. (A special shout-out to "my guy" Tyler. Thank you for being there for my girl and coming as soon as she called. You will always be forever Fave.)

To CJ: I don't even know how to put into words how much I love you. When we met back at the Barnes and Nobles in 2009, I had no idea our life journey would take us all the places we've been. You hold me up and hold me down and know me, the real me, better than anybody on the planet. It still amazes me that God knew back then that I would need you right now, and I am forever grateful. Thanks for being the Ace to my Deuce. I am peacock proud to be your forever lady.

To My Aunts, Uncle, and Extended Family: Thank you for every phone call, text message, token of love, and prayer. I am because we are. So proud we share branches on the same family trees.

To TiJuana: You've always said that you're the "Gail to my Oprah" but you're so much more than that. Who knew that when you bopped in the media center on the first day of new teacher orientation back in 2005, that you'd end up being one of my best friends, my sister from another mister, my daughter's Auntie, and my Brunch Buddy? There aren't even enough words to explain how blessed I am to have you in my life and in my corner and that's saying something since I know a lot of words!

To Helena: If folks even knew half of the details of our relationship, they'd either laugh, cry, or be amazed. In the words of Forest Gump, you and I go together like peas and carrots. Can you believe it's been almost 20 years since we met that day in church? Over the past two decades you've shown me what love truly means. You're the big sister I always wanted, and I thank God for all that you are and have been to me.

To My Nieces (The Fab Five): Jordan, Jamison, Jaylen, Jensen, Javon, the fact that you call me Auntie brings me such joy. Thank you for being so amazing throughout all of this. You've never once made me feel self-conscious about anything and I love you for that.

To Madison: Maddy, I have been smitten by you from the minute I first laid eyes on you. When your mom brought you home, we'd just sit and stare at you because, in our eyes, you were just perfect. You've persevered through a lot during your young life, but you have always shown a strength and a resiliency that most adults would be envious of. But it's your faith, through it all, that I am most proud of. When I was at my lowest, I would think about you and say to myself, "if Maddy can push through, so can I." I love you MaddyCakes and I will always be your Aunt Tristella.

To Aseelah and Jenelle: A 12-day trip through Europe with 36 kids just brings people together, doesn't it? Thanks for every prayer, every encouraging text, every hug, and every "you go girl." Thanks for being a part of my Sister Circle.

To Igola and Mama Dot: Westlake brought us together almost 20 years ago and God saw fit for that to just be the beginning. Thank you for being my arms and my legs when I didn't want the help and for pushing and praying when I needed it.

To CeCe: You told me years ago that God had placed my name in the wind. This isn't how I thought it was going to happen, but the words you spoke over me are indeed coming to pass. Thank you for being that light amid the darkness and for always staying true to your faith and your purpose.

To Candice: Thanks for always checking the weather…(smile)

To Libya: "But as it is written: 'Eye has not seen, nor ear heard, nor has it entered into the heart of man the things which God has prepared for those who love him." You started me on this leg of my journey back on January 1. My cup runneth over.

To My Entire Westlake Family, Past and Present: Thanks for never letting me forget "Once A Lion, Always A Lion."

To My Line Sisters and the Sorors of The East Point/College Park Chapter of Delta Sigma Theta Sorority, Incorporated: Sisterhood is more than just a word. It's a lifestyle. Thank you for all your love and support. So proud to be a part of the BEST Chapter in the Whole-Wide-World!

To My Entire AME Family, Both Near and Far: The Bible declares that the prayers of the righteous availeth much and I am a testament to what this means. Special thanks to the Bishop of the 6th Episcopal District, aka MY Bishop, Bishop Reginald T. Jackson and Supervisor Christy Davis Jackson, Esq. for all your love and support.

To The Embassy ATL: Thanks for letting me be a member in abstention (smile). Apostle Hardin, thank you for always being a blessing to both me and my family.

To Every Single One of My Students: Now, I'm not even going to start calling names because I don't want to forget anyone but if I taught you, if I knew you, if you ever hung out in my room, you're my kid and I thank you for cheering me on. Some of the best motivation for me to keep moving forward is knowing you're watching. I hope to continue to make you proud.

To Eric and Bethany: My Dream Team. I wouldn't have been able to write the last chapter of the book without you. Thank you for believing in what others said was impossible.

And finally,

To Every Single One of YOU: Thank you! Whether you've been following my journey from the beginning or you came in midway, I appreciate every message, like, love, and/or share of God's story. We've only just begun so I hope you stay along for the ride!

The Beginning Before The Beginning

Will Your Heart and Soul Say "Yes?" You Already Have

My husband is the pastor of an amazing church about 20 minutes away from where we live. It's not only the church where he got his start in ministry, but it is also the church where we got married almost a decade ago. It is full of some the most kind, loving, and genuine people I've ever met and it's my favorite place to be on a Sunday morning. Today, as I was sitting in service, the choir began singing one of my favorite songs, "Yes" by Shekinah Glory Ministries. If you're unfamiliar with this song, here are just a few of the lyrics:

Will your heart and soul say yes?
Will your Spirit still say yes?
There is more that I require of thee
Will your heart and soul say yes?
Now will your heart and soul say yes?
Will your Spirit still say yes, yes?
If I told you what I really need
Will your heart and soul say yes
Say I'll obey Jesus
I won't stray Jesus
But this time I've made up in my mind
I've made up in my mind
I'll say, say, say yes

My soul says yes

My mind says yes

My heart says yeah, yeah, yes I will Jesus

Yes, Yes

I'll do what you want me to do

I'll say what you want me to say

I'll go, if you lead me, if you lead me

If you lead me, if you lead me, if you lead me, I'll go, oh, oh

Lift your hands and tell the Lord yes

As they sang, I found myself singing along because, well, that's what you do when you hear a song that you know and like. You sing along. But it wasn't long before I stopped singing. On purpose. Why? Take a good look at the lyrics. A GOOD look. Notice anything?

*Will your heart and soul say **yes**?*

*Will your spirit say **yes**?*

But this time I've made up in mind

I'll say yes

My soul says yes

My mind says yes

My heart says yes I will Jesus

Remember when I told you I said "yes" to God without looking at the fine print? And then I said **we** do that type of thing all the time, agreeing to stuff without knowing what we're agreeing too? Well, let me present to you Exhibit A.

I can't tell you how many times I found myself singing this song in church, in my car, in my living room, everywhere, just a-crying and a-wailing.

"Yes Lord! Yes! To Your will! To Your way! Yeeeessss!"

Un-huh.

So, color me surprised when God took me at my word.

Oh, I hear you. It was just a song! I was just singing a song! Yeah. That's what I thought too, but it was when I was lying in bed in my hospital room that it hit me. I wasn't **just** singing a song. I was making a declaration.

Face Palm

I started thinking about all the praise and worship songs I'd ever sung and came to the realization that even though I didn't know what I was saying "yes" to when I was chillin' in eternity, I confirmed that "yes" with every song I sincerely sang or prayer I sincerely prayed. "Lord, I'll do whatever You say if You just…" **Whatever You Say**. Am I the only one who's ever uttered these words? If you've ever needed a miracle, a breakthrough, an answer to a serious question then I highly doubt it. At the time of our petition, we believe that whatever we're asking God for is the most important thing we'll ever ask God for because in that moment, it is. But what we fail to realize (and yes, I said **we** because we're all in this thing together) is that when we say things like "I'll do whatever You say" He doesn't always brush it off as just something we say. Nope. Sometimes, He takes our "I'll do whatever" as our agreeing to…whatever. Whether we're saying it in a prayer or singing in a song I believe He looks down and says, "Well she said 'whatever' so let me see something." Y'all…

Here's a few lyrics from another song I love, Oceans by Hillsong United:

Spirit lead me where my trust is without borders
Let me walk upon the waters
Wherever You would call me
Take me deeper than my feet could ever wander
And my faith will be made stronger
In the presence of my Savior

In case I forgot to mention it, I'm a former high school English teacher so I have an appreciation for words and word choice. You see those two bold lines, *take me deeper than my feet could ever wander, and my faith will be made stronger*?" Do you know what that is? It's a command. This isn't a suggestion folks. You aren't saying, "Hey God. If You're not busy, might you consider…" Nope. What you're saying is "I want You to take me wherever You need to take me so my faith can be increased." In other words, you're saying "yes."

So, does this mean you should stop singing, or praying, or telling God you'll do whatever. Nope. I started singing the song again and kept on singing just as I had before. The difference is I sang with a better understanding of what my "yes" might entail. And one thing I know for sure, it will absolutely require more strength than I ever thought I had. Guess it's a good thing that when you say "yes" to God, He provides you with everything you need and then some. So, let's dive into this journey together and see what we can discover.

The Intro

I've been procrastinating for weeks.

Everyone said, "you're writing a book, right?"

"When's the book coming out?"

"You need to write a book!"

Yeah. Right.

What if I don't want to write a book?

What if the last thing I want to do is relive the most traumatically devastating moment of my entire life?

What if the sheer thought of reliving each moment makes me want to throw my computer?

Any of y'all buying me a new one if I do?

Let's get this straight once and for all.

I DON'T WANT TO WRITE THIS BOOK!

There. I said it. And yet, here I am, still typing because whether I want to write this thing or not it's not up to me. I don't get a say so. I don't get to look at this journey and decide to keep it to myself. I don't have the right because it's not my story to tell. It's His. Besides, I signed up for this. Yeah. I know. Who in their right mind would sign up for any of this? Good question. According to a friend of mine, me.

I am who.

How does that even make any sense? Another good question, so let me explain.

Jeremiah 1:5 says *"I knew you before I formed you in your mother's womb. Before you were born I set you apart and appointed you as my prophet to the nations."* (NLT)
The CRLT (Chantrise Real Life Translation) puts it like this, *"God said 'Let me holla at you for a minute. You know I've known you forever, right? Before you were even thought of,* ***I*** *knew you. We go way back. And I decided a long time ago that you were the one I wanted to speak to the world."*

Now, because God doesn't force us to do anything, **and** we have free will to say "yay" or "nay" to whatever He asks, **and** I'm sitting here writing a book I don't want to write about a situation I don't want to relive CLEARLY, at some point, somewhere in eternity, he asked and I said "yup." Now mind you, I don't recall signing on the dotted line and I surely don't remember agreeing to any of this but if I'm here and I'm typing and I'm working my way to the other side of through, the only plausible explanation is I gave a head nod, a thumbs up, a fist bump, a high five SOMETHING that God interpreted as the spiritual equivalent of clicking the box next to the word "yes." And do you know why I don't remember any of this? Because God didn't actually **tell** me what my "yes" would entail. Right. I said "yes" without looking at the fine print, not that there **was** fine print but if there had been, I would've overlooked it.

Don't look at me like that.

We say "yes" to things all the time without understanding what we just said "yes" to. And you know what would happen if we really understood what we were saying "yes" to? We'd probably say "no." In fact, many of us would say "no" preceded by any number of curse words. God knows this, which is why he doesn't fill us in on all the details especially when it comes to the plans He has for our lives. **Jeremiah 28:11** says, *"'For I know the plans I have for you' declares the Lord, 'plans to prosper you and not to harm you, plans to give you hope and a future.'"* (NIV)

Notice it says that HE knows the plans He has for you, not that He's going to share them. He already knows us well (remember, we go way back) so laying out for us what we will have to endure in order to possess the blessings He has for us isn't the best idea.

We don't like struggle.

We don't like pain.

We don't like anything that is going to stretch us or make us uncomfortable or inconvenience us. We get irritated when someone cuts us off in traffic or gets our coffee order wrong so He's definitely not going to say something like "I have so many blessings stored up for you! And oh, by the way, when you turn 45 you're going to have a heart attack and lose parts of both your legs."

Yeah. Wouldn't have gone over very well.

But that's not your truth. It's mine.

It's the story you'll read about in this book I didn't want to write. It's the story of the lessons I learned about myself, and about God, and about myself and God together, and family and friends and disappointments and strength and triumphs and failures.

It's the story God chose me to tell, the story I agreed to tell, the story I would've said "no" to had I known better because this story is hard and it's ugly. But, it's also beautiful in a way that I couldn't have imagined when it began.

I thought long and hard about the format for this book and decided I didn't want it to be a simple autobiography. I wanted this to be relatable, for you to connect with me, and find yourself in these pages. My story may not be your story, but I suspect some of this will sound familiar. We aren't that different, you and I, and sometimes, as we are saying "yes" to things we don't understand, we need to know that we are not alone, that there is someone else out there who "gets it."

Each chapter will focus on an aspect of my story that relates to one of the letters in the acronym SHOES (Strength, Hope, Obstacles, Encouragement Success). And because I am a former English teacher who loves a good piece of fiction, the end of each chapter will also introduce you to a Biblical woman who exemplifies each of these characteristics but her story will be set in our present age. These "**Sister Stories"** attempt to make these women and their journeys accessible and relatable to your life.

I will also leave you with a list of points to ponder called **"Think on These Things"** which are thoughts and scriptures that are drawn from the chapter. Some are questions, some are statements, but they were all created to give you something to mediate on throughout the day. *Finally, whatever things are true, whatever things are noble, whatever things are just, whatever things are pure, whatever things are lovely, whatever things are of good report…think on these things.* Philippians 4:8 (NKJV)

And finally, there are two appendices: 1) **The SHOES Playlist** that was compiled with the help of many of my friends on Facebook (yes, you can find me there). It's a list of Gospel songs you can find on Google, or on You Tube, that corollate to each of the five subjects in the book. Never underestimate the power of a good song to help you through. 2) **The Marathon Continues** which is just a way for me to catch you up on all the things I've been doing since the beginning of the year and the end of chapter five.

All in all, this book is the manifestation of my response to God. It is my firm belief that whatever we go through is never solely for us. It's almost always for **someone** we haven't met yet. Why? Because God knew you before you even knew you and he knew that you were going to experience something(s) that were going to shake you to your core. He knew you would need another person who could empathize and/or sympathize with you.

See, He loves you so much, he carried a perfect stranger through something she didn't even realize she had signed up for just so she could write a book she didn't want to write so you could read it and be encouraged. So, I said "yes" because He asked but I also said "yes" for you.

Hey Someone.

Nice to meet you.

Chapter 1

You Weren't Built For This

Oh my God! I wouldn't have made it had it been me!
GIRL! You were built for this!
God gave you this mountain because He knew you could handle it!
God won't EVER give you more than you can bear!
Uggggghhhh. Just go ahead and add these lovelies to the "Stuff I Can't Stand to Hear" list.
Oh, there are others on the list, but these, THESE are the ones I hate the most. Why?
Because I'm not strong.

Not by any stretch of the imagination am I close to **anything** even resembling strong. Folks say stuff trying to be supportive without really understanding what they're saying. See, when people say these phrases, or the myriad variations thereof, they make it sound like I had some level of strength before everything that happened to me that qualified me for this and I assure you, nothing is further from the truth.
I'm a wuss.

Anybody old enough to remember a movie called *An American Tail*? It was about a mouse who was emigrating from Russia to America and got separated from his family along the way. Every time the commercial would come on, little Fievel Mousekewitz could be seen frantically searching for them and then, toward the end, in his squeaky mousey voice, he would say "I'm coming Mama!"

Tears. Instantaneously.

Now, I'm the one on Facebook crying at the posts about animals being rescued or audition videos from America's Got Talent or children saving their allowance to support Veterans. That one post where the little Black girl is adopted by her White foster parents and she cries when she finds out? Complete meltdown.

So, when people say I was built for this I politely, and adamantly, disagree. No one is built for this, least of all me. Now, you might be asking what exactly is the "this" I keep referring to. Well, let me get you up to speed.

On March 23, 2018, I woke up with severe chest pains. My first thought was, "what did I eat yesterday?" I figured it was just gas stuck in my chest as a result of me eating something I had no business eating (no matter how ooey gooey delicious it was. Okay. It was a cheesesteak.). So, I did what any person who lives in Atlanta with gas/heartburn/indigestion would do.

Go downstairs and get a Red Rock Ginger Ale.

If you aren't from Atlanta, or the South in general, Red Rock Ginger Ale straddles the line between beverage and medicine. It's delicious enough to drink as a soda but it has a bite that lets you know it isn't playing any games.

So, I got out of the bed and headed to the stairs, but before I got there, I immediately felt nauseous. I ran to the bathroom and threw up nothing but bile. As I crawled back into the bed, my husband looked at me and asked what was wrong.

"I'm having chest pains. I'm sure it's nothing. I'll get up in a minute." The longer I lay there the worse I felt and finally my husband asked if he needed to call 911. Normally, I would have said "no" because I was notorious for going to work when I was sick but this time, something in my spirit said, "yes."

When the paramedics arrived, they asked my husband what was going on. He told them I was having chest pains. They took my blood pressure and then asked which hospital he wanted them to take me to, so he gave them a name. One of them looked at my husband and said, "If we take her there, she won't make it." To understand my response, you have to understand me.

"I won't make what?"

"To the hospital. You're having a heart attack ma'am." I just looked at her, still experiencing pain in my chest, and said "Oh. Well I guess we need to go to the hospital, huh?"

"Yes ma'am, we do." So off we went.

They loaded me into the ambulance and the last thing I saw was my husband standing outside the ambulance getting ready to get into his car. They gave me a nitro glycerin pill to put under my tongue and I remained conscious during the ride. The next thing I consciously remember is being rushed into the emergency room and seeing my husband standing outside the door.

After that, I don't remember anything until I regained consciousness, what I later found out to be, four days later. During that time, I was told, I died nine times and had to be revived. I was in such bad shape that I was bleeding out, but the doctors couldn't figure out from where. My mother told me that she watched as they kept giving me blood transfusions but as fast as they would give them to me, the blood would rush out. When they tried to move me, the bleeding would get worse and all she could think was her only child was going to bleed to death in front of her eyes. But God…

Finally, from what I've been told, a doctor came in and nixed whatever orders had been given and issued new ones. Whatever he said or did, worked. The bleeding stopped and I was stable.

Once I was released from ICU and moved to a floor, the cardiologist came to see and with tears in his eyes. He said, "if

I didn't believe in God before, I certainly do now. You are a living testimony."

For days, nurses, other doctors, security guards, custodians, everybody, all came by my room just to look at me and tell me how good I looked. (I assure you. I didn't look good in the traditional sense of the word. I looked like I had been to hell and back because that's exactly what had happened.)

I would later be told that three other people, all men, came in the same night as me with the same type of heart attack. It's called a "widow maker" because a) it usually only happens to men and b) if they are married their wives become widows because they die. Sadly, I was the only one who survived.

I ultimately spent two months recovering in the hospital during which time it occurred to me that I couldn't move my legs. I was told I would regain movement once I was strong enough to start physical therapy, so I trusted my physicians and just chalked it up to part of the healing process (I'll share that part of the story later in the book).

About a week into my stay, along with a lot of other issues, I was retaining a lot of fluid so one of my doctors decided to wrap my right leg to help reduce the swelling. I had a few spots on my legs where I'd lost some skin due to the procedures performed to save my life, but other than that, my leg looked normal.

My toes on the other hand were completely black and the tissue was dead. I was told they would have to amputate them. The same was true on my left foot. My mother immediately went into research mode to learn more about prosthetic toes and I was in good spirits

. If all I lost were a few toes, but I still had my life, I was okay; until I wasn't.

A day later the wound nurse came in to change the bandage on my right leg. When she unwrapped it, and removed the gauze, the entire left side of my calf fell off.

Yes. That's what I said. It fell off. I have pictures. You don't want to see them.

I looked at the wound nurse. The wound nurse looked at me and both of our faces said, "I'm pretty sure that wasn't supposed to happen." She called one of my doctors who walked in the room and immediately gasped and put his hand over his mouth.

Me: If you're gasping that can't be good.

Him: Uhhhh… (Eyes wide, hand still over his mouth)

Me: So, how do we fix it?

Him: Hold on. (Leaves room)

He didn't return but an infectious disease doctor did, and he explained that they needed to get blood work done immediately. I wasn't excited about this because all of my veins had collapsed when I had my heart attack. I went from having veins that were easy to find to veins that were non-existent. You couldn't see them, and most nurses couldn't find them which meant drawing blood took an expert's expert. After many sticks and a host of ugly looks from me they got the blood drawn and sent it off to be tested.

It was less than an hour before a vascular surgeon came into my room along with the infectious disease doctor and said, "you have a serious infection in your leg and we're going to have to perform a guillotine procedure to keep it from spreading."

Now, if you reach back to your memories from European History, then you are familiar with what a "guillotine" is. Marie Antoinette was separated from her head using one. The procedure they had to do was in a similar vein. They were going to just cut my leg off below the knee. I looked at him and blinked.

"Huh?" I was okay with a few toes, but this was something completely different.

"We need to do it first thing tomorrow so the nurses will come in the morning to prep you for surgery." I was still blinking.

"Wait. What?" He explained again what was getting ready to happen, but I still didn't quite understand how I came in for a heart attack and I was now facing an amputation. I was training for the Peachtree Road Race, the largest 10K in the world, before all this happened. An amputation was not part of the training plan. But my mother, true to form, did more research on prosthetics and the doctors assured me I would walk again so there was no need to worry. I wasn't so sure but if it needed to be done to save my life, I was okay.

I went in for the procedure and woke from surgery missing my leg below the knee. The doctors left it uncovered so it could drain. My then 20-year-old daughter was fascinated. The rest of us were devastated. My husband and I had prayed. Our friends had prayed. We had called on the prayer warriors in our circle and they had prayed. We read scriptures, and quoted scriptures, and reminded God what He said in His Word. We did all of it believing He was going to save my leg.

He didn't.

So, there we were looking at God genuinely confused and baffled. Hadn't we done everything right? We sought God for answers, and He was silent. The quote that says "the teacher is always silent during the test" kept looming in my mind. My mother, however, was resolute, and essentially told

us to get ourselves together.
"Chantrise is more than just her legs!" Yup. She got us straight right quick and, even though the situation was dire, we fixed our faces and looked forward. I WAS more than my legs, much more, so we decided it was going to be okay; again, until it wasn't.

The next day, the infectious disease doctor came back and ordered more blood work. Again, I gave the nurses all the attitude I was feeling and waited for the results. When the vascular surgeon came back, he looked at me and said stoically,
"The infection is still spreading. We're going to have to amputate your leg above the knee." I took a deep breath and let out a cry.
This was NOT going to be okay.
My mother still wasn't budging, and she rallied the troops.
"We're family and we will all get through this together." Easy for her to say. She still had both her legs! I went into a depression but realized there wasn't anything I could do to change it, so I began to ask God all the questions you'd expect someone to ask in this moment.
"Why?"
"Why me?"
"Why now?"

"What did I do?"

"Why are You punishing me?"

"Are You even listening to me?"

Silence.

I went in for my second procedure and came out missing my leg below my mid-thigh. The first time I looked down and saw what remained, I covered it back up with a blanket and cried. I began to imagine that this is exactly what Jesus was feeling when He was on the cross and cried out "Father! Father! Why have you forsaken me?!" I was lying in bed convinced I was no longer on His radar, and if I was, **He** wasn't the least bit concerned. As far as **I** was concerned, I was on my own.

****

I'm going to stop there for now, even though there is much more to tell, so I can go back to where I started: complaining about people.

You might be looking at me funny through the pages of this book and thinking, "what does she **mean** she wasn't strong? She certainly seemed strong! If that had been me…"

Don't say it.

For the last time, I.AM.NOT.STRONG.

Don't believe me? The Bible even says so.

In the Book of Ecclesiastes, Chapter 3, Verse 20, King Solomon says, "…we all came from dust, we all end up as dust." (MSG) It doesn't get much more plan than that. Dust isn't strong. It's dust and that's how God made us so I can't be inherently strong. Period. Need more proof? Check out the following scriptures:

Philippians 4:13*: I can do all things through* ***Christ who strengthens me****.* (NKJV)

Psalm 18:1: *I love you, God.* ***You make me strong****.* (MSG)

1 Peter 5:10: *And the God of all grace, who called you to his eternal glory in Christ, after you have suffered a little while,* ***will himself restore you and make you strong****, firm and steadfast.* (NIV)

Isaiah 41:10*: Fear not, for I am with you;*
Be not dismayed, for I am your God.
I will strengthen you,
Yes, I will help you,
I will uphold you with My righteous right hand. (NKJV)

1 Chronicles 16: 11: ***Seek the Lord and His strength****;*
Seek His face evermore. (NKJV)

Notice anything interesting? In each of the above scriptures, it is made abundantly clear that we don't have any strength because if we did, we wouldn't have to ask for it. 1 Chronicles 16:11 tells us to **seek** the Lord and His strength. That's a command.

Translated: "Go find God and get some of that strength. You ain't got none."
Isaiah 41:10 quotes God as saying HE will strengthen us. Philippians 4:13, Psalm 18:1 and 1 Peter 5:10 ALL declare that **God** will make us strong so how people assume I had all of this "God-given" strength is beyond me. But…

These same scriptures also show something else. The strength we desire and need only comes either WHILE we are going, or AFTER we have gone, through the fire. 1 Peter 5:10 is very clear, "…**after** you have suffered a little while, [God Himself will] restore you **and** make you strong." Isaiah 41:10 tells us not to fear or worry because He is with us and will strengthen us which is God's way of saying, "I got you."

And He has us because we don't and can't have ourselves. We're just dust, remember? This is not to say that dust isn't useful (Author Lysa Terkeurst speaks about how God uses dust to accomplish His will in her book *It's Not Supposed to Be This Way*. Mind blowing stuff.) but it can't be strong unless it is made strong. And how do we become strong?

Romans 5:3-4: *"We can rejoice, too, when we run into problems and trials, for we know that they help us develop endurance. And endurance develops **STRENGTH** of character, and character **STRENGTHENS** our confident hope of salvation."* (NLT)

So, in order to gain strength, we must run into "problems and trials." When I was a teacher, I used to ask my students how many of them were athletes. Usually a fair amount would raise their hands. I would then ask them how many of them stretched during practice or before it was time for them to compete.

All their hands would go into the air. Then I'd ask, "Does it always feel good?" Their heads would shake "no."

"But is it necessary if you're going to get better as an athlete?" They'd reluctantly nod "yes." I am constantly amazed how my words come back to bite me in the rear.

The word stretch means simply to extend beyond a set boundary and what happens when we don't stretch? Right. We encounter "problems and trials." As a species, we aren't too keen on anything that makes us uncomfortable or painful, so we don't always like to be stretched. When we **are** stretched its almost never at our request but it's so we can develop spiritual strength. God allows it for reason.

Back to my dust example. Do you know how to make clay? Take the right dust and add water. It then changes consistency and becomes a stronger substance that can be stretched and molded into something that can be cured (tried) in the fire which makes it even stronger. Through the process, the dust is transformed into something that can be used or admired.

Do you see where I'm going with this?

When you're faced with problems and trials, ask yourself, "am I being stretched? If I am being stretched, for what purpose is God strengthening me for? How does God need to use me?" See, that's the other part of this. When I was in the hospital, I spent a lot of time singing in the "Woe is Me" Choir. So much so, one night one of my nurses sat in my room and said, "Instead of asking 'why' and 'why me' you need to be asking 'what' and 'who for'." She eventually became my favorite nurse and we're good friends now, but that night, if I had a set of shoes, I would've thrown them at her.

I hate to tell you this, but it has been my experience that when we experience challenges, it's almost never for just our benefit. It's usually for someone else also and often it's for someone we haven't even met yet. That's right. We are being strengthened and stretched and tried and challenged for the purpose of helping someone else fulfill the plans God has for them. Their purpose is divinely tied to us. Doesn't seem fair, does it, that we should suffer for the benefit of someone we don't even know?

Why does that story sound so familiar…

So, will I continue to disagree when people tell me I'm strong to have gone through this?

Yes.

But, instead of rolling my eyes, I will offer a gentle correction. I was **not** strong enough to go through this. I was MADE strong BECAUSE I went through this.

And I was made strong for a purpose.

And my purpose is tied into your purpose.

And your purpose is tied to someone else's purpose.

And so on.

We must be strong enough to endure this race we're running. It's a marathon and for us to run the race we've been given we must build our strength.

Our purpose, someone else's purpose, depends on it.

THINK ON THESE THINGS...

We aren't inherently strong. Our strength comes from God.

- The strength we desire and need only comes either WHILE we are going, or AFTER we have gone, through the fire.
- Take the right dust and add water. It then changes consistency and becomes a stronger substance that can be stretched and molded into something that can be cured (tried) in the fire which makes it even stronger. Through the process, the dust is transformed into something that can be used or admired.
- When you're faced with problems and trials, ask yourself, "am I being stretched? If I am being stretched, for what purpose is God strengthening me for? How does God need to use me?"
- We are being strengthened and stretched and tried and challenged for the purpose of helping someone else fulfill the plans God has for them. Their purpose is divinely tied to us.

Ecclesiastes 3:20: *"...we all came from dust; we all end up as dust."* (MSG)

Philippians 4:13*:* *I can do all things through Christ who strengthens me.* (NKJV)

Psalm 18:1: *I love you, God. You make me strong.* (MSG)

1 Peter 5:10: *And the God of all grace, who called you to his eternal glory in Christ, after you have suffered a little while, will himself restore you and make you strong, firm and steadfast.* (NIV)

Isaiah 41:10: *Fear not, for I am with you; Be not dismayed, for I am your God.*

I will strengthen you, Yes, I will help you,

I will uphold you with My righteous right hand. (NKJV)

1 Chronicles 16: 11: *Seek the Lord and His strength; Seek His face evermore.* (NKJV)

Romans 5:3-4: *"We can rejoice, too, when we run into problems and trials, for we know that they help us develop endurance. And endurance develops* ***STRENGTH*** *of character, and character* ***STRENGTHENS*** *our confident hope of salvation."* (NLT)

SISTER STORIES STRENGTH

A Mother's Love

2 Samuel 3: 7, 21: 8-11

"So, what exactly are you going to do about it?" Rizpah turned around in surprise.

"Debbie! I forgot you were even here."

"Where exactly would I be, Riz? You didn't really think I was going to let you go through this alone, did you?"

Rizpah sighed heavily. It felt like someone had filled her chest with concrete. She struggled to breathe.

"They didn't deserve this Deb. They didn't deserve any of this! They were good boys. They were MY boys!" Deborah placed her hand on Rizpah's shoulder.

"They were my boys too Riz," she said softly. Rizpah sunk down further in her chair and began to cry.

"Here," Deborah passed her a cup. "Drink this. When was the last time you ate?" Rizpah held the cup in her hands and watched as her tears mixed with the peppermint tea she was given. She sighed again.

"I don't know. I'm not hungry."

"Well, you have to eat something, especially if we're going to execute whatever you have planned." Rizpah looked up at Deborah who was now sitting on the sofa next to her.

"What do you mean 'we?' This isn't a 'we' thing Deb. **I** have to do this. I want to do this, by myself." Deborah rested her chin on her hands.
"Oh yeah? You think so? Look. I know you're all Ms. Independent and whatnot but this isn't the time for all that. You aren't doing this by yourself Riz. Besides, I know you. No telling what kind of foolishness you done thought up!"
"Foolishness?! What do you mean foolishness? I haven't even told you what I'm going to do and here you come talking about its foolishness!" Rizpah folded her arms and frowned. Deborah smiled inwardly. She loved her best friend dearly, but she also knew that she wasn't in her rational mind. Afterall, what mother would be after finding out her sons were executed for a crime they didn't commit.
****
"Mrs. Saul ben-Kish? I need you to open the door, ma'am." Rizpah went to the door.
"Who is it?"
"Ma'am, this is the APD. I need you to open the door." Rizpah looked at the doorbell camera and could clearly see a uniformed officer standing at her threshold. She opened the door.
"Yes? How can I help you?"

"Good Evening ma'am. My name is Officer A. Messenger and I have two warrants for your sons' arrest." Rizpah was startled.

"Warrants? Arrest? For what?!" The officer held tightly to the papers in his hand.

"I'm not completely certain Mrs. ben-Kish but I know it has something to do with their grandfather." Rizpah could feel the room start to spin.

"Their grandfather? Saul has been dead for weeks now. What could they possibly have to do with their grandfather---." The officer cut her off.

"Ma'am. I don't have time to explain. I just need them to come with me immediately. Are they here?" Rizpah thought about lying and telling the officer "no" but figured that would just cause more trouble. She looked up at the officer, tears welling up in her eyes and quietly said "yes."

The officer, seemingly unmoved by her tears, asked "well, where are they?" Rizpah called for her two sons. As they came downstairs from their rooms, she asked the officer if her sons were the only ones he was coming to get.

"Yes ma'am. Another officer is at Saul's other daughter's house gathering his other grandsons." Rizpah felt a wave of nausea wash over her.

"Well, when can I come and see them? When is their first appearance before a judge? I need to make sure they have bail money." The officer looked at her stoically.
"I'm sure someone will let you know." Officer Messenger and his partner handcuffed her sons and led them away. Rizpah tried to give them both a hug and a kiss goodbye but they were moving too quickly. She stood at the doorway and watched as they were placed in the car and drove away. She took a sharp breath and went to sit on her sofa. Her heart was running a sprint in her chest. Who could she call?
She jumped up and grabbed her phone. She scrolled through her contacts and found what she was looking for. She pressed the call button and waited. After a few rings, a familiar voice answered.
"Hello?"
"Michael! This is Rizpah ben-Kish. How are you?" Michael was one of Saul's closest associates who also worked at the county jail.
"Hi Mrs. ben-Kish. I'm doing well. What can I do for you?"
"Michael, the police just came and picked up the boys. I need to know what's going on. The officer said it had something to do with their grandfather." She could hear the phone go silent.

"Michael? Hello? Are you still there?" Michael took a deep breath.

"Yes ma'am. I am. So, they came for them too?" Rizpah responded,

"Yes! So, you already knew that they came for his other grandsons?'

"I just found out about them. Didn't know about your sons until now." Rizpah was frantic.

"What's going on? Do you know? I need to get them an attorney. When do you think they'll see a judge? How will I know when to be there? How much do you think their bail will be? Should I come to the jail now or---" Michael interrupted her.

"Mrs. ben-Kish slow down. Don't do anything yet. Let me figure out what's going on. Is this a good number to reach you?"

"Yes."

"Okay. Let me do some digging and I'll get back to you in 48 hours." Rizpah was incredulous.

"48 hours?! I can't wait 48 hours to know what's going on with my boys! I need you to do better than that!' Michael interrupted her again.

"Ma'am, they haven't even been booked yet. I have to wait until they go through the process, but I will say this. It's Friday and they probably won't go before a judge until Monday." Rizpah's heart sunk.

"Monday? My boys can't be in jail until Monday! They won't survive until then!"

"Mrs. ben-Kish, I promise I'll find out some information for you. In the meantime, I'll do my best to make sure they are safe." Rizpah got quiet.

"Okay," she whispered. "Thank you."

"You're welcome ma'am."

"Michael?"

"Yes ma'am."

"Don't forget to call me back as soon as you hear something."

"No ma'am. I won't."

Rizpah hung up the phone and went to sit back on the sofa. Nothing about this was good. What could they have possibly done? She looked at the phone in her hand and called her best friend, Deborah.

"Hey Sis. What's up?" Rizpah felt a catch in her throat.

"Debbie. They came and got the boys."

"Who?! Who came and got the boys?!"

"The police Debbie. The police came and got my boys!" Rizpah began to cry uncontrollably.

"Hold on Sis. I'm on my way."

For two days, Rizpah and Deborah waited for Michael to call.

"It's taking too long Debbie. It's taking too long." Rizpah hadn't slept any and was steadily pacing the floor.

"Riz. You have to get some sleep so you can be ready to move when Michael calls and tells you what needs to happen next."

"I can't sleep, not until I find out what exactly is going on."

At that moment, the doorbell rang. Rizpah and Deborah looked at each other and then at the door. Rizpah stood completely still. The doorbell rang again. Deborah walked to the door and opened it. Michael was standing outside.

"Hey Mike," Deborah said.

"Hey Deb. Is Mrs. ben-Kish home?" Rizpah slowly turned around

"I'm here Michael." He nodded his head at Deborah and walked into the room.

"Have a seat," she said. Michael looked anxious.

"I'd rather not ma'am." Rizpah sat down on the sofa. Deborah sat down next to her.

"So, the fact that you're here…you could've called. Why didn't you just call?" Rizpah looked up at Michael, but her heart already knew why he had come by.

"Michael, what's going on with my boys?" Michael took a deep breath.

"Saul was like a father to me. If anyone was going to come to you, it had to be me so I got permission to come." Rizpah felt a sharp pain in her chest.

"What's going on with my boys, Michael?" He looked her in the eyes.

"There was a riot ma'am. All seven of Saul's grandsons were killed." Rizpah blinked a few times and held her breath.

"What do you mean, they were killed? Michael, what do you mean?!" Rizpah began to breathe again, but much more rapidly.

"I tried my best to make sure they were in as safe a place as possible after they were booked. In fact, I was able to get all seven of them in the same area together. I figured they could be each other's support while they got through the weekend." Michael paused and took another deep breath.

The first night was fine, but earlier today, a few of the other inmates approached the boys and asked if they were Saul's grandsons. They said 'yes.' They proceeded to tell the boys that Saul had broken a promise to their father and disrespected him. They boys said they didn't know anything about that and tried to walk away. Another of the inmates grabbed one of your sons and said he needed to pay for the promise his grandfather broke. It went downhill from there.

They began fighting and soon it wasn't just Saul's grandsons and the other inmates. It was everyone in the cellblock."

Rizpah barely heard anything Michael said. All that kept ringing in her ears was "all Saul's grandsons were killed."

"But Michael, they weren't supposed to be there in the first place." Rizpah felt nauseous again. "Why were they even picked up in the first place?"

Michael shifted his weight from one leg to the other and looked at the floor.

"Apparently, Mrs. ben-Kish, Saul was involved in some, uh, interesting business transactions and when it came time for him to supply the names of those people who would be responsible for the fulfillment of these transactions if he was no longer around…he named all seven of his grandsons."

Rizpah held her head in her hands.

"Interesting? You mean illegal." Michael responded.

"Yes ma'am." Rizpah took a slow deep breath.

"So, my sons, and his other grandsons, were picked up and sent to jail for something they didn't do, something they didn't even know about?" Michael looked at her quietly.

"Yes ma'am." Rizpah rubbed her forehead.

"Michael, how did they die?" Michael stuttered.

"Ma'am. I don't think you really need to know the details---"

Rizpah stood up and yelled.

"HOW DID THEY DIE?!" Michael took a few steps backwards.

"They were stabbed to death ma'am. Once it was over, the inmates said the debt had been paid."

Rizpah could barely breathe. Michael continued.

"I was told that they died defending each other. They were very brave." Rizpah fell back on the sofa and laid her head back. Staring at the ceiling she asked,

"When can I see them? Where are their bodies?"

"The county morgue ma'am." Rizpah sat back up.

"Thank you, Michael. You can leave now." Michael paused for a moment.

"I'm very sorry for your loss, ma'am." Rizpah slowly shook her head as she watched Michael walk out of the door.

****

"So, what's the move?" Deborah leaned forward on her knees and grabbed a tissue and gave it to Rizpah.

"I'm going to the morgue."

"Correction. **We're** going to the morgue." Rizpah looked at Deborah.

"What part of **I** are you having such difficulty with?" Deborah looked back at Rizpah.

"The part that doesn't include **we**. You're not going by yourself Riz. I don't care what you say. Besides, you don't even know how long it will be until they release the bodies." Rizpah slowly leaned back on the sofa.
"It's doesn't matter. I'll be there for as long as it takes. I couldn't be there when my sons died but I surely will be with them now. I want to see what they're going to do to my babies"
"First off all, I don't even know if you can be in the room while they're doing the autopsy. Second, I don't think that's what you need to see. Remember them as they were, Riz, not as they are now. Third, you can't stay up all night watching and waiting. I'm coming with you, that way if you doze off, I can keep an eye on things. I don't know how long this will take but I'll bring snacks and blankets and some bottles of water. I'm here with you Riz and I love you until further notice."
Deborah put her arm around Rizpah's shoulder and pulled her in close. Rizpah wept in Deborah's arms.
"We'll leave first thing in the morning and we'll stay for as long as it takes, okay?" Rizpah sniffled.
"Okay."
Deborah passed her another tissue.

“You know you don’t have to do this, right?” Rizpah sat up and blew her nose.

“Yes Debbie. I do. I was strong for my boys when they were alive, and I will be strong for them now that they are gone.”

Deborah looked in admiration at her friend. “Clothed in strength you are indeed my friend. Clothed in strength you are indeed.”

Chapter 2

Surrender

May 31 marks some pretty amazing events. Supposedly, in 1279 BC, Rameses II (Rameses The Great) became pharaoh of Ancient Egypt. (How anyone knows that for certain is beyond me but so sayeth Google.) In 1969, John Lennon and Yoko Ono recorded "Give Peace a Chance" and Stevie Wonder released "My Cherie Amour." In 2008, Jamaican Sprinter Usain Bolt broke the world record in the 100m sprint with a time of 9.72 seconds and in 2018, my husband turned 44.

It also happened to be the day I finally left hospital #1 to head to hospital #2.

Rehab.

This was the day I had been waiting for. I was going to spend the next three weeks working extra hard so I could strengthen my legs and get ready to receive my prosthetics. Afterall, every doctor I had encountered up to that point had told me not to get discouraged with my progress because 3 weeks of therapy in the rehab facility was going to get me what I needed. For the first time since March 23, I felt something new.

Hope.

I have a friend of mine who, when wondering how I am doing asks, “How’s the weather?” During the 71 days I was in the first hospital, my responses sounded like monsoon season in West Africa.

Gloomy. Gray. Stormy.

Some days I would say it was partly cloudy but for the most part I was Seattle on steroids.

The day I left for rehab was a physically sunny day as well as a metaphorically sunny one. I felt better emotionally than I had in months. Hope had clawed her way up and over every piece of bad news I’d received and was standing proudly on the rubble that was my reality in full superwoman regalia.

Hands on hips, chin thrust forward, red cape billowing in the wind.

Ta Da!

It was a glorious feeling but, by definition, that’s kinda what hope is.

Hope (noun): *the **feeling** that what is wanted can be had or events will turn out for the best.*

Another definition says that hope is,

an optimistic attitude of mind based on an expectation or desire.

For the first time in what felt like an eternity my attitude was one of optimism and not despair. I threw my entire self into being positive. I was ready!

The Bible talks a lot about hope by the way. In fact, it's mentioned 129 times.

One of the more familiar passages is **Jeremiah 29:11:**

"For I know the plans I have for you," declares the Lord,

"plans to prosper you and not to harm you, ***plans to give you hope and a future."*** (NIV)

The Message Bible says it like this,

"...I know what I'm doing. I have it all planned out---plans to take care of you,

not abandon you, ***plans to give you the future you hope for****."*

God and I still weren't on the best of terms. I was still angry that I was an amputee. I was still angry that my legs weren't working properly, and I was downright ticked off that He still wasn't answering any of my prayers. One of my failings, by the way, is that I hate to be ignored.

By anybody. Most of all, God.

But, because I was determined to see the positive side of all of this, and scripture DID say that He would give me the future I hoped for, I decided that God didn't have to speak to me. He could show He was still real by simply doing what I asked.

Allow me to walk again in the three weeks I was in rehab.

I was looking for a supernatural healing, an encounter that would completely restore my belief in Him. That's all I wanted. I wasn't asking for too much. I mean, He was God.

All mighty.

All powerful.

All of that.

Getting me back walking was an easy task compared to other things He had to handle on earth.

Easy Peasy.

But how many of you remember what I said in the previous chapter? That thing about God allowing us to experience challenges for the purpose of stretching and strengthening us?

Yeah. I didn't remember either.

So, when, in less than 12 hours after my arrival, I found myself in another ER, would you like to guess how I responded?

Yup.

Full out, over the top, ugly attitude, with a great big capital "A."

The reason why I was back at yet another ER, had to do with the massive hole in my left foot due to necrotic tissue that had been removed ("necrotic" is just a fancy word for "dead."). The wound nurse at hospital #2 discovered that said wound was not healing properly and more tissue had died so I needed to be evaluated by another doctor to determine if I needed to have another surgery to clean it all up.

Again.

And, joy of joys, when I was finally seen by a doctor (eight hours later), he smiled and said,

"Well, I don't think you need any additional surgeries. We just need to see how things progress."

Yay! No new surgeries.

"But, if it doesn't start healing on its own, you're going to need another amputation."

Have you ever been in a fight and been punched really hard in the stomach?

Me either. But I'd watched enough Rocky Movies to decide that what I felt at that moment had to have been 10x worse.

And the expletives I let loose as a result surely would have had me at the altar for the next year and a half had I let them leave my brain and exit my mouth.

But I didn't. I was too busy crying again.

And that wouldn't be the last time I cried during my three-week stay either. Or the last time I cussed. Or the last time I felt betrayed by God. I would leave the hospital still not able to walk, still an amputee, and still with a large open wound in my left foot. Emily Dickenson wrote a poem called "Hope" is the thing with feathers, an extended metaphor that likens hope to a bird that continues to sing even when times get rough. My bird, as far as I was concerned, had flown the coop.

Now I realize my story is nothing like yours, but I also know I'm not alone in my feelings of disappointment when things continue to NOT go the way you planned, when the hope you had just ups and walks out like a 90s R&B song. And that's when good ol Jeremiah 29:11 starts to get on your nerves.

Okay. My nerves but I'm sure I'm not alone in this feeling either.

"For **I** know the plans **I** have for you," declares the Lord…

Yeah. That part.

Our plans aren't always His plans and He's under no obligation to share His plans with us. The fact that He knows what those plans are should be enough. Should be. It's not.

Can I be honest? I like being in control. I like knowing exactly where I'm heading, AND I like knowing how I'm going to get there. You'll never see me hop in my car and just drive off into the sunset for kicks and giggles.

Nope. Won't be me.

But if you happen to be one of those people who is totally okay with everything that happens in your life and you never question God or what He's doing or why He's doing it, I applaud you. Really. I do. But I have a very tangible fear of being lost and not knowing what God's plans are for my life feels a lot like taking a road trip without using the Waze app on my phone.

But then the Bible says,

"…plans to prosper you and not to harm you, ***plans to give you hope and a future.***" (NIV)

Let's do a quick word study. Any idea what a **plan** is?

A specific project or definite purpose; an arrangement or intention.

Any idea what the word **definite** means?

Clearly defined or determined, not vague or general; fixed; precise; exact."

"For I know [**the exact purpose**] I have for you," declares the Lord,

"[**a precise intention**] to prosper you and not to harm you, [**a fixed arrangement**] to give you hope and a future." Jeremiah 29:11

So, He may not give us the specifics, but He makes it very clear that there is a method to the madness. Everything that happens to us is for a specific reason and that is to give us hope and a future.

Read that again.

Everything that happens to us is for a specific reason and that is to **give us hope and a future.**

So, all this stretching we're doing is so God can **give** us strength but also so He can **give** us hope. The fact that it must be given means we don't already have it. Just like strength, we only get hope as a result of an experience we deem difficult. If we don't ever experience challenges, there's no need for us to ever experience hope. Think about it.

If everything in our lives is going well, what do we need to hope for?

Exactly. Nothing.

But knowing all of this doesn't make reaching hope any easier than gaining strength does. Either way, we have to go through somethings in order to reach what's on the other side. But that's not all. Do you know what else we must have to have hope?

Faith.

When used as a verb, **hope** means,

To believe, desire, or trust; rely; ***to have faith in***

Hebrews 11:1 says,

Now faith is the substance of things hoped for, the evidence of things not seen. (NKJV)

Essentially, faith and hope are different sides of the same coin. Faith believes it is so now, while hope believes it will be so in the future. Regardless, both require us to put our trust in what we cannot see.

Faith. Hope. Trust. They all go together.

And since we're already knee deep in all of this, let me go ahead and put the icing on the proverbial cake by telling you the final thing we must do to get hope.

Surrender.

A little while back I mentioned that I like to be in control. I want to do what I want, when I want, and how I want. I want to know how things are going to go before I start and I want to know how, and when, things are going to finish. This made me the ideal patient, of course. There's nothing doctors and nurses like more than a patient who's a control freak with a superiority complex.

The truth is, had I let go of my need for control, I probably wouldn't have been so miserable. It's hard to stay positive and hopeful when you're too busy being angry because you're not the one calling the shots.

As an only child, I've always been the independent type. Because it was usually me, myself, and more of me, I learned to be self-sufficient. I didn't ask for help because I didn't want it. I saw it as a sign of weakness. Like many only children, I longed to be part of a group, but I also enjoyed being alone. The term "introvert" hadn't made its entrance into our collective lexicon yet, but I was definitely that. But, it was my need for control that proved to have some potentially deadly consequences when I was around 16.

One Saturday afternoon, I was in the kitchen making myself something to eat at our gas stove. I turned away to grab something off the opposite counter and instead of turning back around, I backed up too close to the stove and my shirt caught on fire. I screamed as loudly as I could and before I knew it my father was bounding up the stairs from the basement coming to my rescue. To this day, I have no idea how he managed to get my shirt off and over my head without recreating Michael Jackson's 1983 Pepsi commercial, but he did. As I stood there in my bra, stunned, my father wrapped his hand in a cold towel and told me he was going to the emergency room to have his hand looked at. Before he left, he looked at me and asked,

"Do you know what you said when you were on fire?" I quickly raced through my memory, hoping I didn't say a curse word or two.

"No. All I remember was yelling for help." He frowned slightly.

"Actually, you didn't say anything. You yelled but the words 'help' never came out of your mouth." I thought that couldn't possibly be true. Who finds themselves on fire and doesn't ask for help?
Me.

If I didn't ask for help and I was on fire, how likely do you think it was that I was going to ask for help while I was in the hospital? I couldn't do anything on my own. I couldn't use the bathroom or bathe without assistance. I couldn't get out of the bed unless I was carried, and I couldn't roll over without the nurses doing it for me. I would cry every time I had to be bathed and I chose to do without a lot instead of asking for help with anything. At the rehab hospital, my bed had an alarm that would sound loudly if I even attempted to get out of the bed. As far as I was concerned, I was being held hostage. I had no say so in when I woke up, when I went to bed, when I ate, when I went to therapy, when the doctors came, or when they left. I spent so much energy fighting against the support I was angry all the time.
And as you have probably already figured out, I was angriest at God.

Not just because He had taken my leg and my mobility, but because he had taken away my independence and that was the worst part of it all.

I didn't speak about God. I didn't speak to God. I didn't pray. I didn't praise. I didn't believe. I didn't hope, and I surely didn't trust. I held on to every negative thought and feeling as proof that everything I thought I knew about God was a lie. But you know that scripture, Proverbs 22:6:

Train up a child in the way that he should go,
And when he is old, he will not depart from it? (NKJV)

That's real because even though I was angry there was still a small part of me that knew, deep down inside, that He was still real, just like I had been taught. Hope, that thing with feathers, was trying to sing. But what was it going to take to get God back in my good graces?

Yup. I had to surrender.

On a particularly bad day, the chaplain stopped by to see how I was doing. She didn't know I was having a bad day but everything in my face made it very clear. She sat in my room for a little while and asked me a few questions. I gave her the shortest answers I could come up without appearing rude. After a few minutes she asked,

"Have you told God how angry you are with Him?" I looked at her, confused.

"What do you mean?"

"Have you told God how you really feel?" Again, I was puzzled. Why would I need to tell God how I felt? He was

God. Clearly, He already knew.

"I know what you're thinking. Why would you need to tell God something He already knows? Well, it's not for Him. It's for you."

When speaking about forgiveness, Bishop T.D. Jakes says "I think the first step is to understand that forgiveness does not exonerate the perpetrator. Forgiveness liberates the victim. It's a gift you give yourself." Letting go of anger works in the same way. I couldn't receive the hope I so desperately needed until I was able to be honest about how I really felt. I had to let go of the anger and the need to be in control so I could receive what He wanted me to have.

I looked at her as tears welled up in my eyes. She walked over and patted my hand before she prayed with me. When she left the room and I was alone with my thoughts, it felt like my throat was closing. The tears flowed warm down my cheeks and I took a deep breath.

"God," I whispered, "I hate You."

Yes. I know. Who am I to say I hate God? The God who sees the bigger picture. The God who created me. How dare little insignificant me say that to God Almighty!

Well, before you judge me too harshly think about this. If you're a parent, have you ever done something your child didn't like and they folded their arms, frowned, and said "I hate you?" They didn't mean it any more than I did but it's how we felt. And guess what? It's perfectly okay to express our feelings to God, even if what we're expressing is anger. The Bible is replete with folks who were angry with what God was or was not doing. We're not the first and I assure you we won't be the last. The Apostle Paul even tells us in **1 Corinthians 10:13**,

Sometimes it will be difficult for you not to do something wrong. Or it will be difficult not to think something wrong. You will have difficulties like this.

But they are the same kind of difficulties that every person has…

(EEB2018: Easy English Bible)

Did hope miraculously show-up after I unburdened myself? Nope. But what did happen was I stopped barricading the door with pent up anger and I allowed God to begin the process of healing my heart.

Notice I said, "begin the process." This surrendering thing wasn't instantaneous. Letting go of my anger was just the first step. It would take many more months before I would hear myself utter, "not my will, but Yours be done." But, as I often tell people, baby steps are still steps, and slow progress is still progress.

So, when we're looking for hope, the first thing we need to do is figure out what we must let go of. What's blocking God's ability to give it to us? It's a small but important step but what's that saying, "a journey of a thousand miles begins with a single step?" Well, life **is** a journey, so we need to start somewhere!

THINK ON THESE THINGS…

Hope can only manifest after we surrender.

- Everything that happens to us is for a specific reason and that is to give us hope and a future.
- Just like strength, we only get hope as a result of an experience we deem difficult. If we don't ever experience challenges, there's no need for us to ever experience hope.
- If everything in our lives is going well, what do we need to hope for?
- It's perfectly okay to express our feelings to God, even if what we're expressing is anger.
- When we're looking for hope, the first thing we need to do is figure out what we must let go of. What's blocking God's ability to give it to us? It's a small but important first step.

Proverbs 22:6: *Train up a child in the way that he should go,*
And when he is old, he will not depart from it? (NKJV)
Jeremiah 29:11: *"For I know the plans I have for you," declares the Lord,*
"plans to prosper you and not to harm you, plans to give you hope and a future." (NIV)
Jeremiah 29:11: *"…I know what I'm doing. I have it all planned out---plans to take care of you,*
not abandon you, plans to give you the future you hope for." (MSG)

Hebrews 11:1 *Now faith is the substance of things hoped for, the evidence of things not seen.* (NKJV)

1 Corinthians 10:13: *Sometimes it will be difficult for you not to do something wrong.*

Or it will be difficult not to think something wrong. You will have difficulties like this.

But they are the same kind of difficulties that every person has… (EASY)

SISTER STORIES

HOPE

A Woman Called Hope

1 Kings 17:7-24

"Momma, I'm hungry."
"I know baby. Momma's going to make us something to eat."
She watched as her son scampered off to play before she turned her gaze to the kitchen.
"Momma's going to make us something to eat" she said again, this time in a whisper barely audible to herself.
"There isn't anything to eat" she sighed.

Hope had been sitting at the table by the window staring outside when her son, John, ran into the room. He was such a happy boy, a handsome boy, even though he had a Jack-O-Lantern smile characteristic of children his age. He'd spent most of the summer running around outside with his friends, so his complexion had darkened from its usual pecan color to a deep mahogany. His head, full of sable curls, was in serious need of a shape up, so much so that she made a mental note to ask a friend if she would braid it in cornrows just to keep it neat.
He looked just like his father.

She knew she needed to take him to the barber, but she didn't have the money for that. In fact, she barely had any money at all.

Hope continued looking in her kitchen at the cabinets that were bare, except for a near empty container of oatmeal. She sighed heavily again.

"This would never have happened if Josh was here" she thought. "We never had to want for anything, but now…" Her voice trailed off and cracked as she could feel the tears welling up in her eyes.

Josh was Hope's husband and the love of her life. High school sweethearts, they met in the ninth grade in their Honors Algebra class and became rivals almost immediately. Math was Josh's best subject and Hope's favorite subject, so they were always in competition to earn the highest grade in class. In the beginning, Josh sat directly behind her because the teacher placed the students in alphabetical order but that didn't last long. Whenever the teacher asked a question or wanted someone to work out a problem on the board, Josh would make a point to try and push Hope out of the way which meant she **had** to push back in response.

It got to be so bad that eventually Josh was moved to the other side of the room to avoid any further conflict. Their tenuous relationship continued until their Junior year when they found themselves co-captains of the debate team… and Josh asked Hope to the Junior Prom. They'd been together ever since.

Hope wiped the liquid grief from her face. "You're still supposed to be here. This wasn't how our story was supposed to end," she said.

It had been a year since Josh's death, and she was struggling to make ends meet. She had been a stay at home mom when Josh was alive because it was important to them both that she stayed home with John until he was ready for kindergarten. When that time came, Hope decided she didn't want to go back and work a traditional 9-5. She wanted to have a schedule flexible enough to allow her to be home when John got out of school. Uncertain what she wanted to do, she and Josh decided it would be best for her to take a year to explore a few options and see which one fit best.

At the beginning of John's first grade year, Hope decided that she wanted to offer coding classes to the students in her neighborhood and had started reaching out to various schools to determine their interest. The response was extraordinary, and she was on her way home to prepare her proposal for John's elementary school when she got a phone call. It wasn't a number she was familiar with but something in her gut told her to answer. All Hope could remember was a man telling her she needed to come to the hospital immediately. There had been an accident.

Everything after that was a blur. None of it seemed real, and it wasn't until she had to pick out the clothes Josh was to be buried in that it hit her. He was gone, and with him every dream they'd had for the future.

Hope grabbed a napkin and wiped her face as she stood up and walked into the kitchen. Josh had a life insurance policy, but it was just enough to cover the funeral expenses. She still needed money for she and John to live off of, so she took out a modest loan with the expectation that she would be able to find a job that would allow her to pay it off quickly. While she was able to find a job, it didn't pay as much as she would've liked or needed, especially when the landlord raised the rent on their townhome. The increased rent and the loan payments were a strain on her budget. Add to that after-school care for John, utilities, groceries, car payments, gas, and Hope had begun to lose what she had left of her name.

Eventually, the money from the loan ran out and she was unable to keep up with either the loan or car payments, so she went into default and the car was repossessed. Without the car, she couldn't get to work so she was let go. She was able to collect unemployment for a little while but that ended also and when she applied for food stamps, she was told that she needed to show that she was actively looking for a job in order to receive them. One of her neighbors suggested she ask for assistance from the local church, but Hope didn't like that idea. She didn't believe in God and she certainly didn't trust a man who claimed to speak for Him. Besides, if God was real then Josh wouldn't be gone, and she wouldn't be standing in her kitchen trying to figure out how to feed her child. "Mooooomaaaaaa," John yelled from his room, "when are we gonna eat?" Hope didn't have the strength to say anything other than, "soon."

She opened the only cabinet that had anything in it and took the container of oats off the shelf. There was just enough for her to make a small bowl for John and an even smaller bowl for herself. "After this, there isn't anything else," she said out loud. "We're going to starve to death."

The thought was terrifying, but she had used up all her resources and her options. "Maybe I should go to the church," she thought but then decided against it. Hope ran some water into a pot and sat it on the stove. "John! I'm running outside to grab the mail, okay? I'll finish making dinner as soon as I come back in." John ran out of his room and hugged her leg. "Okay Momma. I love you," and then ran back to play with his Legos. She could feel her chest tighten. It is not supposed to be like this…

Hope opened the door and walked the short distance to her mailbox. "Maybe I'll have a mailbox blessing," she thought. She opened the door and laughed quietly as she used the phrase her mother used to explain the unexpected arrival of money. No money ever arrived unexpectedly at their house growing up, but her mother said it just the same. She just shook her head.

"Ma'am. Ma'am?" Hope turned around to see a vaguely familiar face.

"Yes?"

"Uh, hi, yes, my name is Elijah. I'm the pastor of the church down the street." Hope just looked at him and blinked.

"Hello."

"Yes. I hope I'm not bothering you, but I was wondering if you had a snack to spare." Hope wasn't certain she heard him correctly.

"A snack?"

Elijah continued. "Yes. A snack. I know this sounds a bit odd, but I was doing some work at the church and I started feeling light-headed. I'm a diabetic and in the rush to get out of the house this morning I forgot to bring something with me to eat."

Hope just stood there looking at him thinking "I KNOW this man didn't just ask me for something to eat. I KNOW he didn't."

"I'm sorry, what did you say your name was? Elijah? Yeah well, I don't have anything for you to eat. I have just enough for me and my son and after we finish that there won't be anything left." She turned around and proceeded to go back in the house.

"Ma'am?" Elijah called again. "I understand, but if you would just make me a little before you make something for you and your son, I'd be so very grateful." Hope stopped, squared her shoulders, and turned back around.

"Excuse me," she said incredulously. "Did you just ask me to give what little I have left to you first?"

"Yes ma'am. My sugar is getting low and I just need a little something to get it back right." Hope looked him in the eye.

"Have you lost your mind?? I'm not giving what little I have left to a perfect stranger! Did you not hear me? I have just enough for me and my son and once that's gone, we're going to die. Do you hear me? Die!" Hope spun back around, completely disgusted by Elijah's request. She started to walk away, grumbling under her breath when she heard Elijah speak again.

"I understand ma'am, but God told me to tell you that if you feed me just a little of what you have, neither you nor your son will ever go hungry again." Hope stopped again and turned around. Just as she was getting ready to read him from Genesis to Revelation, she noticed that he was slightly swaying, as if he would pass out at any moment. She looked at him and sighed.

"Come on in."

Elijah followed Hope into the house, and she pointed to the chair she had been sitting in previously.

"Have a seat. All I have is oatmeal," she said.

"That sounds wonderful," said Elijah. Hope looked at him briefly and rolled her eyes. What was she doing? There wasn't enough for all three of them.

Hope prepared the oatmeal and made Elijah a small bowl. Then she made one for John and called him to come and eat. John bolted out of his room and stopped when he saw Elijah.

"Hi!" he said. "I'm John! What's your name?" Elijah smiled.

"My name is Elijah."

"Hi 'Lijah! Are you here to eat too?" Elijah smiled again.

"Yes I am. Your mother invited me." John smiled broadly.

"My momma is the bestest isn't she?" Elijah looked up at Hope and said "The bestest!"

John grabbed his bowl and began eating. Elijah began eating as well. She leaned against the door jamb for a moment before turning around to scrap the last little bit of oatmeal out of the pot. When she looked inside, she squinted in confusion.

How was there enough oatmeal in the pot for her to have a full bowl? She walked back into the room and looked in John and Elijah's bowl. They were still eating but she knew there was no way they could still be eating and there be enough in the pot for her. She looked back at the pot again and then looked at Elijah. He looked up from his bowl and said,

"I feel so much better now. Thank you. Aren't you going to eat?" Hope just stood there.

"Hope? Are you all right?" She blinked a few times.

"How do you know my name? I didn't tell you my name." Elijah took a napkin and wiped his face as he settled back in the chair.

"God told me your name, the same way He told me to come down the street and ask you for something to eat." Hope just stared.

"Huh?"

"You came out to the get the mail and halfway expected a 'mailbox blessing.' Instead of that, he sent me; And because you gave me part of what you had, God says you'll never have to worry about being hungry again." Hope continued to stand there confused and baffled by what she was hearing when John spoke up.

"We won't ever be hungry again? Really? Does that mean we can have waffles for breakfast??" Elijah laughed.

"I suspect you and your momma can have whatever you like."
"Yay!" yelled John. "Momma, when can we go grocery shopping? Now? Can we go now??" John was out of his chair jumping up and down in front of her. Flustered, she responded.
"John calm down. Calm down! We can't go grocery shopping without any money so unless Mr. Elijah has some, we won't be going anywhere." Hope turned her gaze back to Elijah.
"Why would you say something like that? Something you can't back up. It's just wrong to lie to a child, and to me. What kind of pastor are you?!" Elijah responded.
"One who believes in God." Hope stared back at him.
"Oh yeah? Well Mr. 'I Believe in God' how do we go grocery shopping with no money?" At that moment there was knock at the door.
"Hi! My name is Josh with Amazon Fresh with a delivery for, uh, Hope?" Her voice quivering, she said,
"I'm Hope, but I didn't order anything from Amazon Fresh. What did you say your name was again?" He smiled.
"My name is Josh ma'am. I have an order here for you. In fact, according to my records, you're supposed to have groceries delivered to you once a week." Hope's eyes widened.
"What do you mean? I didn't order anything!"

Josh looked at his tablet. "No ma'am you didn't but someone did and its already been paid for. So, where would you like me to put the bags?" By this time, John had come to the door to see what was going on.
"Ooooo! Groceries! Are there any waffles in there??" Josh the delivery guy responded.
"Yup. I believe so. You wanna show me where to put them? They're frozen and I don't want them to thaw out." Josh said
"I'll show you! Hey 'Lijah! We have groceries!" Elijah smiled.
"Oh yeah? Imagine that." Hope shut the door and just looked back at Elijah who was looking at John show Josh the Delivery Guy where everything should go.
"Elijah," Hope said, "How?" Elijah chuckled.
"God." Hope felt the tears streaming down her face.
"But I don't believe in God." Elijah looked up.
"You don't?"
Hope stuttered. "Well, I-I-I didn't used to. I mean I do now, but I didn't when you came up to me."
"Then why did you agree to feed me?" Hope thought for a moment.
"I don't know. You were ill and I felt as if I had to help you."
"Hmmm. Well look at that. You didn't believe in God, but you agreed to help someone who does. As a result, my prayer for something to eat was answered and your prayer for

something to eat was answered as well." Hope sat down.
"Yeah. I guess so." Hope looked over her shoulder at John who was still in the kitchen with the delivery guy. He was holding a box of waffles over his head dancing and singing. "I got waffles yes I do! I got waffles how 'bout you?!" Hope laughed to herself, looked up toward the ceiling and said "Thanks Josh." The delivery guy came out of the kitchen.
"No problem! It's my job. I'll be back with the rest of your bags in a minute." John ran after him and said, "I'll help!" Elijah stood up and walked toward the door.
"So…might I see you on Sunday? God does a lot more than just provide groceries." Hope smiled.
"I think we'll be able to make it."
"Good. Service starts at 10:00. I'll see you then. Oh, and Hope?"
"Yes?"
"Don't stop believing, okay?"
She looked up at him and said,
"I won't."

Chapter 3

This Doesn't Feel Like Victory

You ever fervently pray for something to happen, and then when it does you realize you're not actually ready for what you prayed for? That was me a week before I left rehab. Aside from a short visit to the hospital garden, the trip from Hospital #1 to Hospital #2, and a brief field trip to the local Panera Bread, I hadn't been outside since I was carried to the ambulance on March 23, 2018. I literally watched the weather change through the windows in my hospital rooms. I used to cry as I thought about the entire world going on about their business without me. I was jealous of my friends and family who would come to visit and then could just leave whenever they got ready. Afterall it was Spring/Early Summer in Atlanta which means it was the beginning of Patio Season. I wanted to be able to leave too!

What is Patio Season you ask? Patio Season is the time of year when the weather is consistently warm and beautiful and every restaurant with a patio, deck, or outside seating is full of people who made it through the Atlanta winter season without being stuck on a major highway during an ice storm. And I was missing all of it.

I wanted to be sitting somewhere with the sun in my face drinking a mimosa. Or at least that's what I thought I wanted. The truth is, I was still uncomfortable being seen in public without my leg (I hadn't had my second amputation yet). I was bloated from my body retaining water, my signature platinum blonde hair had long since grown out and been cut off, my perfectly manicured fingernails were non-existent, and my once confident persona had been obliterated. In my mind, I saw myself as I once was. I was no different than I had always been, but one look in the mirror, reminded me of all that I'd lost. I didn't really want to be sitting on a patio with the sun in my face. What I really wanted was my old life and the old me, back. Neither was going to happen.

So, when one week before I was to be released from rehab, my physical therapist decided I was going to practice using my wheelchair outside on the sidewalk in front of the hospital I cringed. Not only was there a busy street in front of rehab but there was also a bus stop, and a shuttle stop for the doctors and nurses, and there were college students, and patients, and a whole host of random strangers, all of whom would be staring at the bloated, bald headed, fingernailless, amputee, in the wheelchair.

I don't remember if I mentioned his before now, but I'm an introvert. No one believes me when I say that but it kinda comes with the territory when you were raised an only child. I like my space and I don't like people in my space. I also don't particularly care for being in other people's space.

When I want to be social, I can be, but most of the time I like being alone, usually with my nose in a book. The sheer thought of being around a bunch of folks in public made me nauseous. It was going to be way too peopley out there. Nevertheless, there I was staring outside the door waiting to go outside.

"You scared" see asked?

This was a loaded question by the way, and I knew it. Laura (not her real name) had been my physical therapist since I arrived, and she made it very clear that she was going to push me.

"We have goals to meet" she'd always say. "And we don't have time to waste!" My love/hate relationship with Laura was strong. On the one hand, she was kind and encouraging but on the other hand she wasn't listening to any of my excuses either. She poked me in the arm gently.

"Hey. I asked if you were scared."

If I said "yes" she'd just push me out the door and say something like "Good! Let's get over that fear!" If I said "no," she'd say something like "Great! Show me whatchu got!" There was no answer I could give that was going to get me out of the whole, "go outside in your wheelchair and be among the masses" event so I didn't say anything at all. Laura just shrugged and said "Well here we go" as she pushed me out of the door.

Once outside she let go of the wheelchair which was my signal to propel myself the rest of the way down the incline to the sidewalk ahead. She walked beside me as we took a left and went to the next corner, cautioning me to watch out for the dips and divots in the pavement. When we got to the corner, we turned around and headed back to the hospital. I thought to myself that it wasn't so bad. Nobody stared or looked at me funny, so I gave myself a mental pat on the back for my courage. And then…

"You know what? Head to the other corner. I want to see you cross the street." I stopped the wheelchair and looked up at her.

"Ummm, you want me to cross the street?" Laura smiled and started pushing the wheelchair to the crosswalk.

"Yup." The street had four lanes, two going and two coming and was a part of a busy intersection. The crosswalk timer was set at 30 seconds, but this is Atlanta.

Southern hospitality doesn't extend to folks in crosswalks.

If you're moving too slowly, expect to hear a car horn, a cuss word, and/or a hand gesture at the very least. There's a song by a local rapper called "Move" the chorus of which says "Move! Get out the way! Get out the way! Get out the way!"

(If you're reading this and you're familiar with the song then you know these are the clean lyrics).
Pretty sure it's the city's anthem.
Having this on the forefront of my mind, we approached the corner where we were to cross.

I was still building up my arm strength so they were pretty tired by this time and when I looked at how wide the street was, coupled with the speed at which the cars were moving, I just knew I wasn't going to make it across the street in 30 seconds. Laura was unmoved.

"Okay," she said excitedly, "ready, set, go!" I put my hands on the wheels and started propelling myself across the street. I realized that I had more strength than I thought because I got to the other side with 10 seconds to spare; gave myself another mental pat on the back. Now, all I had to do was get back to the other side and I could go take a nap.

If you've never had to use a wheelchair to get around, then you are unaware how much energy it takes. Standard issue hospital wheelchairs easily weigh 30-40 pounds. Add to that your own body weight and your arms feel like warm Jell-O fast. This is especially true after you decided you wanted to audition for a part in the next Fast and Furious movie and sped across the street like you were being chased.

The light changed from green, to yellow, to red and the crosswalk timer began. I tried to kick in the after burners on my wheelchair and realized I no longer had the strength. I struggled to get halfway across the street when my arms just gave out, and there I was, stuck in the middle of the intersection watching the time count down 3…2…1…

I looked in the faces staring at me from behind the windshields and mouthed "I'm sorry" as they crept toward the intersection, and me. Right at that moment, Laura came behind me with a sturdy push and got me the rest of the way across.

There was a lady waiting for the bus and when she saw me, she smiled and said, "Good job!" I smiled back at her. "Thanks," I said softly. I was so embarrassed. How was I ever going to navigate the world outside the hospital by myself? Discouragement came to see about me. Laura, however, was resolute.

"That was awesome! You did it! How'd that feel?" I felt myself roll my eyes.

"I know what you're thinking. **You're** thinking it wasn't awesome because you needed help getting back across the street, aren't you?" I just nodded my head, tears welling up in my eyes.

"Welp," she proclaimed gleefully, "it was still awesome and so were you. I know you were scared, and I know you don't like asking for help, but this really was a huge accomplishment and **YOU** need to be proud of yourself." She pushed me all the way to bottom of the hospital driveway before she stopped and stood in front of me.

"Hey! Hey, you," she tapped me on the forehead. "Did you hear me? Be proud of yourself!" I started to smile.

"Say it. Say, 'I'm proud of myself.' Say it before I start tapping you on the forehead again." I laughed.

"I'm proud of myself." Laura leaned down closer to my face.

"What? What'd you say? I can't hear you." I rolled my eyes and laughed again.

"I **said** I'm proud of myself!" Laura stood up and chuckled.

"Oh, okay. I just wanted to make sure. Now wheel yourself up to the front entrance."

I stopped smiling. The entrance to the hospital, remember, was at the top of a steep incline and, where was I? At the bottom. I moaned. Laura wasn't hearing it.

"Come on now. We don't have time to waste, unless you want to get caught in the rain."

It was then that I saw the storm clouds overhead and began to feel the raindrops. I put my hands on my wheels and started pushing. My arms were on fire but I pushed my way up the hill, around the cars that were parked in the circular driveway, and right when I arrived at the glass doors Laura came behind me and said, "I guess I can push you to your room now. You've earned it." I looked up at her as she smirked.

"Ohhhh, so you're gonna help me now? Gee thanks!" We both laughed as she wheeled me into the elevator.

"But seriously," I said, "Thank you." She patted me on the shoulder."

"You're welcome. You got this."

****

A week later, my husband and my mother came and packed up my room and prepared to bring me home for the first time in 3 months. The day before, they, along with my father, daughter, and best friend, had spent some time with me and my therapists so everyone could see what I was able to do and what I was going to need help with. I was able to transfer successfully from my wheelchair to the car and to the bedside commode. I was also regaining some strength in my limbs. I could sit up without falling over which was huge since for at least two months I wasn't able to. They learned how to get me up and over a curb in my wheelchair and what medicine I needed to keep track of. As I said goodbye to the nurses and the staff, I began to feel anxious.

I was going home.
The home I hadn't been in for 3 months.
The home with two floors, one of which I couldn't reach because I wasn't able to get up the stairs.
The home in my neighborhood where everybody knew me.
The home where I was going to have to relearn independence.

All I prayed for when I was in the hospital was to go home and now that the day was finally here, I was terrified.

One of the challenges you face after spending so much time in the hospital is what I call "learned dependency." There was so much I could no longer do and so much I wasn't allowed to do that I learned to depend more on the nurses and staff and depend less on myself. This was a huge development for Ms. Independent. Clearly, I didn't see my dependency on others as a good thing and I felt like a failure. So, what did I do?
I quit.

Rather than accept the help from my family when I got home, I just stopped doing any and everything that required help. I barely ate and I barely bathed. I slept most of the day and was up most of the night.
Being at home was a nightmare.

Even though my mother had taken it upon herself to completely redo our entire house in preparation for my eventual return by buying new furniture, and new toilets, and organizing every closet and forcing my husband and daughter to throw away anything that was taking up space, all I could think about was what once was…and what would never be again.

I was a miserable woman and I was miserable to be around. God bless my parents and my husband and my daughter. If I didn't know what true love was before then, I surely know what it is now. They **had** to love me because I know most days, I was unlovable. I had a home health nurse who came three days a week to check on me and to change the dressing on the hole in my left foot and I had a physical therapist who came and worked with me trying to further strengthen my legs. But, other than that, I had very few visitors because I didn't want any. I was going to live the rest of my life hold up in the house and simply waste away.

I was now relegated to sleeping on the new sofa my mother purchased and I had to use a portable toilet stationed next to it because my wheelchair wouldn't fit in doorway of the bathroom on the first floor. I bathed on that same sofa using a bowl of warm water and soap and brushed my teeth there also. Everything was a struggle. In the past, when I was irritated or when someone at the house got on my nerves, I would grab my sneakers and go for a run. Now, when folks got on my nerves, I became even more irritated because I **couldn't** just go for a run. I couldn't even leave the house without help. For the next six months it was a battle between my memories and myself. Pastor Joyce Meyers might call this the "Battlefield of the Mind." Truthfully, it wasn't even a battle.

It was an all-out war.

I never felt like I could catch a break because there was always something I couldn't do, always a challenge to overcome. Mind you, there was plenty I **could** do, but when you're trying to recover from a major trauma, and life as you know it has exploded in your face, you don't see the positive progress. All you can focus on is the regression. And I assure you, no one, not one person, faulted me for my almost daily meltdowns. It was expected and it was understood. I mean, how else are you supposed to respond?

Don't copy the behavior and customs of this world,

but let God transform you into a new person by ***changing the way you think.***

Then you will learn to know God's will for you, which is good and pleasing and perfect.

Romans 12:2 (NLT)

While I had many physical obstacles to overcome, my biggest obstacle were my thoughts. I was suffering from what is called a "fixed mindset."

According to Carol Dweck, a psychologist at Stanford University, our mindset is one of the things that helps us decide how we choose to live our lives and determines whether we live one of progression or stagnation.
A "fixed mindset" is exactly what it sounds like, a belief system or attitude that is fixed, immovable, or stuck. If we believe we aren't good at something, we behave in such a manner that pretty much guarantees we will continue to not be good at it because we don't believe it can change. For example, if you want to be a dancer, but you have a "fixed mindset," **and** you are a member of the "Rhythmless Nation," you won't take lessons because you'll feel it's a waste of time.
So, how do we get past these roadblocks? Two words:
Cognitive Flexibility

Now before you get thrown off by this term, let me explain. "Cognitive Flexibility" or "Flexible Thinking" is our ability to adjust the way we think when faced with obstacles we weren't expecting.
It's also exactly what Paul is telling us to do.

Don't respond to issues the way the world does, but instead shift our thought processes so we aren't walking around doing our best impressions of The Grinch. To make it even plainer, when life kicks us in the teeth, we shouldn't run to **things** in order to feel better. We shouldn't run to people either. Or drugs. Or alcohol. Or any host of other things we tend to run to when life sucks. To do this we MUST change our perception of the situation so we can think of some better alternatives.

Don't copy the behavior and customs of this world,
but let God transform you into a new person by ***changing the way you think...***

The International Reader's Version (NIRV) says:
Don't live any longer the way the world lives.
Let your way of thinking be completely changed...

And the Easy English Bible 2018 (EASY) puts it like this:
Do not become like the people who belong to this world.
But let God completely change the way that you think, so that you live differently...

I don't know if you're sensing a common thread in this book yet, but have you noticed that everything I've been able to accomplish thus far is because of Him? God gave me strength. God gave me hope. And God gave me a new mind. There was no way I was going to overcome the obstacles I'd set up in my head without surrendering to His will.

Uh-Oh. There's that word again.

Surrender.

But here's the nitty and the gritty. There is no overcoming, no victory, without surrender. I realize that's a pretty counterintuitive thing to say in the natural world since **surrender** and **victory** don't go together. Can you imagine what would happen if a solider returned from war and, when asked how it went, he replied, "We were victorious General! We surrendered!" Somebody would have a lot of explaining to do. But thankfully, it's not that way in the spiritual world. When we surrender to His way and His will, we get the victory. Period.

But I'm going to tell you this.

It ain't easy.

As we have already established, I am an independent soul who likes to be in control. Now, I realize I'm probably the **only** one who has this issue. I'm sure **you're** perfectly okay not being in control and I'm also certain **you've** never felt angry because you weren't. It's just me.

I know. Pray for me.

But in case you ever come across someone **else** who might be like me there's a few things I'd like you to share:

1) The word **Surrender** means *to give oneself up, as into the power of another; submit or yield.* One of the best examples

of what it means to surrender can be found in Luke 22:42 where we find Jesus in the Garden of Gethsemane:

Father, if you want, you can save me from this time of great pain. But I do not ask you to do what I want. Do what you want for me." (EASY)

The fact the Jesus understood what surrendering meant, that He knew it was not easy, gives me a sense of peace. If **He** had doubts about this whole "let go and let God" thing, surely my concerns are valid. But, that last part, "***I do not ask you to do what I want. Do what you want for me***" is Jeremiah 29:11 personified. He didn't necessarily like the plan God had for His life, but He trusted that whatever the plan, God knew best. I mean, can you imagine if Jesus had decided NOT to trust God's plan? If He told God, "You know what? I'm good. I didn't sign up for this whole 'dying for other people's sins' thing?" What kind of victory would **we** have over the challenges we need to overcome if Jesus' response was "no?" Whew! Sometimes our surrender isn't just for us. It's for folks we haven't even met yet. (Sound familiar?)

2) The word **Overcome** means *to get the better of in a struggle or conflict; defeat*
to gain the victory; win; conquer. It literally means to "come over" something. When I was a runner, the worst races were

always the ones with a lot of hills. Where I live in Atlanta, there are hills everywhere. You just don't notice them because most of the time you're in your car. But let me tell you something, if you're running a half marathon in this city you find out quickly how hilly Atlanta is. Those long gradual hills make you question your very reason for being. They always seem to show up after you've already run 5-6 miles and your legs are telling you to just quit already. While you're running up the hill, your legs are on fire and it's difficult to breathe but you push through because you know what's waiting for you at the top?

Gatorade and water!

Oh…and a nice long decline.
And the opportunity to give your legs a break before, yup, the next hill.

But isn't that a lot like life? We face a challenge and overcome a challenge just to have another challenge we must overcome rise over the next hill. But when it's all said and done, there's nothing like crossing that finish line. I don't care how hard the race was, how much you cried or cussed, when they snap that picture, and give you your medal, you completely forget about all you had to endure to get there. All that matters is this: you made it, and you get to talk about it at work on Monday. James 1:12 says:

Those who stand firm during testing are blessed. They are tried and true. They will receive the life God has promised to those who love Him as their reward. (CEB)

If you don't think running a half marathon (or any race for that matter) is a test I encourage you to go run one. Yes. Overcoming the physical challenges is hard but guess where the greatest challenge is? Right. Your mind. Convince yourself you can't finish the race and you won't. Which brings me to point number three.

3) If we're going to overcome anything, the first thing we must do is change our minds. Earlier, I talked about what it means to have a fixed mindset and how to use cognitive flexibility, or flexible thinking, to get us un-fixed. What I didn't mention is the root of the fixed mentality. Fear. Most of us get stuck because we are afraid of what might happen if we disturb our own universes. What does that mean? Glad you asked!

   In T.S. Eliot's poem "The Love Song of J. Alfred Prufrock," we meet a man who has found himself at a swanky dinner party where the woman he likes is also in attendance. He stands back and watches her as she interacts with other members of the societal elite and is fearful that they will notice the bald spot in the middle of his head or that his clothes are ill-fitting. He questions whether he should enter their circle by asking a simple question: "Do I dare disturb the universe?" In other words, "should I interrupt what they have going on by joining their conversation?" I'm not going to tell you what dear Brother J. Alfred decided to do but I will say this. In order to disturb their universe, he had to first disturb his; i.e. he had to overcome his fear of possible rejection and make his move. So often we don't overcome things because we're afraid of what might happen if we do.

We're in a lousy relationship but we stay because we fear being along.
We don't get the degree because we fear we aren't smart enough to complete it.
We don't start the business because we fear we won't be successful.
We don't go on the date because we fear being let down or rejected.
We don't apply for the job because we fear we aren't qualified enough.
We don't ever move forward in our future because we're afraid of letting go of the past.
We're always sick but we don't go to the doctor because we're afraid of the diagnosis.

We stay stuck because fear has us believing a whole bunch of stuff that's not true. But here's the truth. 2 Timothy 1:7 says:

God has not given us the spirit of fear, but of power, of love and a ***sound mind.*** (NKJV)

God didn't give us fear **but** He DID give us a sound mind, a mind that isn't confused, a mind that doesn't argue with itself, a mind that isn't fixed on what we can't do.

So, here's the end of it all. Folks, if we're going to overcome, changing our mind isn't optional. It's required. But the good news is that we are more than able to do this because we can do all things through Him who strengthens us! (Philippians 4:13)
Change your mind, change your life, and overcome.

THINK ON THESE THINGS...

Change your mind. Change your life. Overcome.

- Don't respond to issues the way the world does. Instead shift your thought processes so you aren't walking around doing our best impressions of The Grinch.
- There is no overcoming, no victory, without surrender.
- If we're going to overcome anything, the first thing we must do is change our minds
- God didn't give us fear **but** He DID give us a sound mind, a mind that isn't confused, a mind that doesn't argue with itself, a mind that isn't fixed on what we can't do.

Romans 12:2: *"Don't copy the behavior and customs of this world, but let God transform you into a new person by changing the way you think. Then you will learn to know God's will for you, which is good and pleasing and perfect.* (NLT)

Don't live any longer the way the world lives.

Let your way of thinking be completely changed... (NIRV)

Do not become like the people who belong to this world.

But let God completely change the way that you think, so that you live differently... (EASY)

James 1:12: *Those who stand firm during testing are blessed. They are tried and true. They will receive the life God has promised to those who love Him as their reward.* (CEB)

2 Timothy 1:7: *God has not given us the spirit of fear, but of power, of love and a* ***sound mind.*** (NKJV)

Philippians 4:13: [We]e can do all things through Him who strengthens us! (Philippians 4:13) (NKJV)

Luke 22:42: *Father, if you want, you can save me from this time of great pain. But I do not ask you to do what I want. Do what you want for me."* (EASY)

SISTER STORIES OVERCOMING

The Challenged Inheritance

Numbers 27: 1-11; 36:2-12

"I hate him!" Tirzah stomped into the house and slammed the door. Mahlah looked up from the dinner she was preparing to see her sister come in from summer camp.

"Girl, what is your problem? Why are you coming in here slamming doors?" Tirzah slammed her backpack on the floor, threw herself on the sofa, and began to cry.

"Tirzi? What's wrong?" Mahlah sat down on the sofa beside her and rubbed her back. Quietly, she said, "Tirzi, talk to me. What happened?" Tirzah continued to cry.

"Sweet pea, I can't fix it if I don't know what's wrong." Mahlah continued to rub Tirzah's back and began plotting who she had to find and hurt for making her little sister cry.

"Tirzi? Come on. Sit up and tell me what's going on." Tirzah did as she was told, her tears leaving long salty trails down her little face. At five years old, Tirzah was far more mature than other kids her age and Mahlah was often told that Tirzah was an "old soul." She often chastised the children in the neighborhood for "crying like babies" so Mahlah was at a loss as to what it was that made her so upset.

"Tirzi, come on now. Calm down," Mahlah whispered, "and tell me what's going on. Who do I have to go fight?" Tirzah turned her face to her big sister.

"Simon. You have to go get Simon!" Mahlah rolled her eyes.
"Lord," Mahlah smiled. "What did Cousin Simon do now? I swear you two get into it at least once a week!"
"He's mean!" Tirzah narrowed her eyes and frowned. Mahlah sighed.
"Well what did he do Tirzi?" Tirzah took a deep breath.
"He said that we're going to get evissted! Mahlah looked puzzled.
"We're going to get what?"
"Evissted!" Tirzah began to cry again and flung herself into Mahlah's lap. Mahlah looked at her lying there.
"Tirzi," she said softly, "I still don't know what you're talking about. Evissted? What does that even mean?" At that moment their sister Holli appeared in the doorway to the room.
"Evicted. She thinks we're going to be evicted." Mahlah stared at Holli.
"Why in the world would she think that?"
"Because she was trying to be all up in grown folks' business **as usual** and overheard a conversation between Mayor Moe and Mr. Eli about who gets to stay in this house and on this land. I swear Tirzi, all that snooping is going to get you in some real trouble one day." Tirzah sat up quickly, faced her other sister, and yelled.

"I wasn't snooping! Simon and I were walking from the bus and Mayor Moe and Mr. Eli were walking in front of us. I heard them talking!" Mahlah looked at Tirzi.

"Okay. You heard them talking. I'll get to that in a minute. Now why are you mad at Simon?" Holli jumped in the conversation again.

"Because Simon started teasing her saying that she was going to be homeless and she got upset." Mahlah frowned at her sister.

"I wasn't talking to you Holli. I asked Tirzi." Holli rolled her eyes and shrugged her shoulders. At twelve years old, Holli was entering her pre-teen years and everything she did and said came with a certain level of attitude.

"I was just trying to help."

"Well you're not so just be quiet." Mahlah turned back to Tirzi.

"Tirzi, honey, I don't know what you overheard but we're not going anywhere. Daddy made sure we had plenty of family to take care of us. We're fine." Tirzi looked up and began to wail again.

"No, we're not! We're going to be homeless and we're going to have to beg on the streets, and no one will ever want us and then we're going to diiiiiiieeeee." Tirzah flung herself back onto the sofa. Mahlah sighed.

"Tirzi,…"

"God! Why do you always have to be so dramatic?!" Holli asked frustrated.

"I'm not being dramatic!" Tirzah hollered. "You're being mean!" Mahlah rubbed the back of her head.

"Alright," she yelled. "Enough! Holli, you shut up, Tirzi you stop crying."

"I heard the same thing ya know." The three sisters turned toward the doorway to the porch and saw their eight-year-old sister Milcah standing there.

"Where'd you come from," Mahlah asked.

"Uh, I'm standing on the porch. Where'd you think I came from?" Mahlah's eyes narrowed in irritation.

"Little girl…. How long have you been out there?" Milcah responded by shrugging her shoulders.

"I dunno. Long enough to hear that we're going to be evicted." Tirzah began to cry again.

"Seeeeee?! It's not just me!" Mahlah sighed heavily.

"Milcah…"

"Everyone's talking about it, how we're going to have to leave," Milcah said quietly.

"For the last time, we're not going anywhere now leave it alone!" Mahlah sighed again.

"Leave what alone?" asked their fourth sister Noah. She was fifteen and had been in her room the entire time and only came out because she heard the commotion.
"What's going on?" She turned and looked at Tirzah, "and what's wrong with her?" Milcah walked over to her little sister, sat down beside her, and then put her in her lap.
"What's wrong Chicken Nugget?" Tirzah began to tell her the story when Mahlah interrupted.
"Not now, Tirzi. It's time to eat. Go get washed up." Tirzi began sobbing.
"But...."
"Come on Tirzi," said Noah who picked her up in her arms, "let's go get cleaned up for dinner. We can talk about it later." Tirzi sighed and nodded her head as the two of them left the room.
"Milcah, help Holli set the table."

Mahlah went back into the kitchen and removed dinner from the oven. It was hard being the oldest of five. Their mother died giving birth to Tirzi and her father raised them until he passed away two years ago when Mahlah was 16. The courts tried to split them up but Mahlah came up with a plan and petitioned on their behalf to not only keep them together but to remain in their family home. The judge was so impressed with her maturity and resourcefulness that he agreed, as long as she had adult family members who were willing to act as guardians. Their father left no will so the five girls were left in the care of the court system and their benevolent relatives. But, based on what Tirzi was saying, it sounded like that was all getting ready to change.

After the sisters finished eating, they sat around the table quietly. Mahlah spoke first.

"Okay. So, let's talk about this. Tirzi says she overheard Mayor Moe and Mr. Eli talking about allowing our house and our land to be taken over by developers. Is that right Tirzi?"

Tirzah nodded her head.

"Yes, and they said we were going to have to leave." Her lip began to quiver. Mahlah grabbed her little hand.

"Calm down Tirzi. Calm down. They said we would have to leave…" Mahlah's voice trailed off as she thought out loud. "Why would we have to leave? We have family that takes care of us when necessary and there haven't been any issues. When I turned eighteen, I became your legal guardians despite what a lot of people said and we're doing just fine. The money that Daddy left covers the mortgage, utilities, and food and I'll be getting a job soon to supplement what other funds we get. While I am thankful for the help from family, we are doing well on our own. Why would they want to evict us?"

"Because the mortgage and the deed aren't in your name," Holli responded as she played with her fork. Mahlah looked at her.
"First of all, who told you that, and second of all it's never been in my name and no one had an issue. Why is it an issue now?" Noah responded.
"Because they want the land Mahlah," Noah replied. "You remember how Daddy used to talk about how long this land has been on our family and that one day someone was going to come along and try and take it from us? That's why it's an issue." Mahlah sighed.
Noah continued. "They think that just because we're girls we shouldn't have this house or this land. It's too valuable and they want it, but it's not theirs to take. This land has been in our family for generations and it's ours. Period."
"But what if no one else feels that way," Holli interjected. "What if they just say 'Hey! They're just a bunch of girls. We can take this land away from them easily and build yet another mixed-use development that will price out everyone in the neighborhood!" Holli's sisters all looked at her.
"What? I read the news on my phone. They're having a city council meeting tomorrow to discuss the new development and the land they want to grab for it." Mahlah just sat and stared at her sister.

"Whaaaaaaat?" Holli asked before rolling her eyes. "You act like I don't know anything. I know plenty of stuff."
Mahlah responded, "Well there's no doubt about that. So, the council meeting is tomorrow, huh? We'll be there. We will not lose this home or this land." Tirzah piped up.
"That's right! Our big sister will tell 'em!" Tirzah smiled for the first time since she came home. "They're not going to evisstecate us!"
"Maybe," Holli pondered, "but I would feel sooooo much better about all of this if I knew they were actually going to listen to Mahlah." Mahlah stood up from the table and began clearing the dishes.
"Us. Listen to us." She carried her dishes back into the kitchen.
'Us? What do you mean **us**? Who's the us?" Noah asked.
Mahlah came back out of the kitchen and grabbed more dishes. "Us Noah. We all have to attend the meeting and speak to the city council if we're going to keep our inheritance."
"Can't you just find a husband," Milcah asked. "I mean, just get married and your husband will take care of us." The sisters looked at the eight-year-old.

"Girl go sit down somewhere," said Holli. "Mahlah isn't trying to be married. Are you?" Holli cocked her head to the side and looked at her sister.

"She's not looking for a husband because she doesn't want one! She has us!" Tirzah announced happily.

"Would y'all just be quiet please? No, I'm not looking for a husband. Yes, I would like to get married one day, but right now we need to focus on what's in front of us and that's making sure no one can remove us from this house or this land." Mahlah continued clearing the table.

Noah looked around the room and grabbed what was left of the dishes and brought them into the kitchen. Mahlah followed her. Noah turned to face her.

"Mahlah, do we really have to do this? You know I hate speaking in front of people. What if it doesn't work." Holli entered the kitchen carrying a fork for the sink.

"Oh, it's gonna work!" Holli punched her right fist into the palm of her left hand. Milcah followed and chuckled at her sister.

"What are you gonna do? Beat 'em up?" Holli narrowed her eyes and made a fist.

"Want me to beat you up instead?" Milcah screamed and ran out of the kitchen with Holli running behind her. Mahlah screamed,

"STOP IT! That's enough!" She leaned against the sink and hung her head.

"Listen. This is what we're going to do. Each of us is going to speak, one after the other, and explain why we should be able to keep our house and our land. Tirzi, you'll go first since you're the youngest and you're cute. People love to listen to cute kids." Tirzah smiled proudly. "After that, Milcah, you'll go followed by Holli, and Holli, don't threaten the people." Holli gave a slight smirk but agreed. "Noah, you'll go next and all go last." Noah frowned slightly.

"But Mahlah, I'm scared. You know I hate speaking in front of people!" Tirzah came up next to her and tugged on Noah's hand.

"You don't have to be scared Noah. Mayor Moe is very nice, and he likes kids! Whenever he comes to visit us at school, he always brings candy and he smiles at us. Please come with us." Noah looked down at the face of her sweet sister and smiled.

"Okay Love Bug. I'll be there."

****

The next morning, the daughters arrived at the City Council meeting and signed up to speak during public comments. When they're names were announced, Tirzah spoke first.

"Hi Mayor Moe! My name is Tirzah." The Mayor smiled sweetly at her.
"Well hello there Tirzah. What can I do for you today?" Tirzah stood up as straight as possible and said, "Mr. Mayor Moe sir, our father died two years ago and left us in the care of our older sister Mahlah and some of our relatives. We're doing fine and want to stay in our house and on our land, please." Tirzah did a little curtsey like she had seen little girls in the movies which prompted a few chuckles from the mayor and those in attendance. Milcah came up next.
"This house and this land have been in our family for a really long time, since the olden days, and we really would like to stay there. Our father loved our house and we loved him so I think we should be able to stay, for him." Milcah bowed slightly. Holli was next at the microphone.

"Mr. Mayor Moe, we know that there are people who want to take our land and our home because they want to build some new mixed-use complex and our house is in the way. I don't care about whatever they want to build. I care about our house and our land and you should to. Remember when you were running for mayor and nobody liked you? Our father was the only one who helped you campaign, and you won.

You wouldn't even **be** mayor if it wasn't for our father so I think you need to tell these developers where to go and how to get there because…" Mahlah hissed at her sister and gave her a look that very clearly said "shut up" so she did and backed away from the microphone. The Mayor smirked.

Noah approached nervously and said, "Mayor Moe sir, it's not our fault that our father died so soon and it's not fair that someone wants to take from us what is rightfully ours." Noah paused. "I suspect we wouldn't even be having this conversation if our father had five boys instead of five girls, but here we are. Prove me wrong Mr. Mayor and allow us to stay where we are." The Mayor shifted nervously in his seat. The developers were sitting, watching, and listening in the council meeting. He had already verbally agreed that he would help them get the sisters land but said the city council had to vote and agree. He looked up and caught the eye of one of them. He was not happy.

"Do you ladies have anything else to say?" Mayor Moe asked. Mahlah approached the microphone.
"Simply put, what we're asking you for is to help us protect our home and our land by telling the developers to find another place to build. There's almost 20 acres of unused

space on the other side of town that would perfect for the type of project they want to build, and it's already zoned for commercial use." The Mayor looked at Mahlah, shocked. She continued.

"I know many people in this room think that because we're a bunch of girls that we couldn't possibly know anything about keeping up a house and maintaining the land. We couldn't possibly know anything about the other business dealings in this town and how this entire deal is about these developers making money at all cost. I mean, that would require a lot of research, fact checking, and digging around and how could we **possibly** have time to do all of that with all of the girl stuff we have to do." Mahlah narrowed her eyes. "I implore you not to make the mistake of thinking we're just a bunch of kids. There's a reason why the judge allowed me to become my sisters' legal guardian at such a young age. Thank you." The Mayor took a deep breath and looked ate sisters.

"We will take a 10-minute recess while we discuss this issue behind closed doors." The Mayor banged his gavel and stood up, but not before he looked at the sisters and then the developers. He sighed again and he and the city council exited the room.

The sisters huddled together and prayed that the Mayor and the other members of the council would decide in their favor. After 10-minutes, they returned. The Mayor banged his gavel.

"After discussing your request with the council, we have decided unanimously, to suspend the petition for construction of the mixed-used development on your land. You may remain in the house and on the land for as long as you are able." The daughters shouted with joy while the developers swarmed around the city council and pleaded their own case. The Mayor banged his gavel once again and said,

"Although this is not customary, we will go into another brief executive session for approximately 10-minutes." He banged the gavel and the council exited again. The daughters looked around the room at the developers.
What was going on? Had the Council changed its mind?

They held hands and prayed again that the Council wouldn't reverse their decision. After what seemed like much longer than 10-minutes, the Mayor and the City Council returned. He banged his gavel again.

"After taking into consideration the considerable money and time the developers have already put into their project, we have decided that you may stay in your home and on your land for as long as you are able **but** if you were to ever decide to sell the house and/or the property the developers would be provided the opportunity to purchase it first. Do you understand?" Mahlah approached the microphone.

"Yes, Mayor Moe, but we won't be selling anytime soon, if ever." Mayor Joe smiled.

"That's fine. Is there anything else?" All the girls stood around their sister.

"No Mayor Moe. Thank you."

"Excellent. We will break for lunch. We will return at 1:00 to continue addressing the other issues concerning the city." The Mayor banged the gavel once more. Tirzah looked up at him and waved. The Mayor smiled and gave her a thumbs up. Tirzah went and slid her hand inside of Mahlah's and leaned against her arm.

"You did it Mahlah." Mahlah removed her hand and put it around Tirzah's shoulder.

"Nope Chicken Nugget, **we** did it." Tirzah smiled.

"Yup. We sure did."

Chapter 4

I Think I Can

When I think about friendship, there are three songs that immediately come to mind. First, the theme song to *The Golden Girls*:

Thank you for being a friend!
Travel down the road and back again!
Your heart is true
You're a pal and a confidant!
And if you threw a party, invited everyone you knew
You would see the biggest gift would be from me
And the card attached would say
Thank you for being a frieeeeeennnnnnd.

Second, "Friends" by the rap group Whodini:
Friends
How many of us have them?
Friends
Ones we can depend on
Friends
Before we go any further, let's be
Friends

And third, my forever favorite, "What About Your Friends" by TLC:
What about your friends, will they stand their ground,
Will they let you down again?
What about your friends, are they gonna be lowdown,
Will they ever be around,
Or will they turn their backs on you?

I'm sitting here typing and singing the lyrics to each one because they are each iconic in their own way. Depending on when you grew up, where you grew up, and who you grew up around, these are all songs I bet you can sing without ever looking up the lyrics. We're talking prime karaoke lyrics here y'all! But they are also indicative of the types of friendships I have in my life now.

If we think of friendship as a set of concentric circles, the TLC song represents the Outer Circle Folks. These are the people who were there long enough to be nosey. The ones who feigned concern so they could get "the tea" on what was going on in my life so they could report back to whomever. You know, people that I'll speak to when I see them in public but who aren't invited to the cookout.

The Whodini song represents the Inner Circle folks, the people who came into my life during this madness and have proven to be folks I can depend on. I not only speak to them, but they can come to the cookout AND bring an appropriate dish.

Now, The Golden Girls Theme Song represents the most important group of people. These are my Sacred Circle Folks, the circle closest to me and my heart. THESE are the people who not only are invited to the cookout, but they'll probably be there the night before helping prepare for the following day, or they'll still be there long after everyone else is gone. They are the people who have either been in my life forever or feel like they have because they have proven time and time again that they aren't going anywhere.

In the Bible, the most sacred place in The Tabernacle is the Holy of Holies, and it's located beyond the veil. The Sacred Circle Folks are my BVCs, my "Beyond the Veil Crew." These people, mostly women, know me so well that I've trusted them with secrets I dare not speak out loud, hurt I can't express, and joy no one else would understand. These people are the ones who cover me in prayer and know how to speak a Word over my life so I can move mountains. They are the ones who have my back.

If you don't have any BVCs, I need you to reevaluate your circle and kick some people out so you can make room for the type of friends you need. When you're going through hell, they're the ones who not only will come and see about you, they'll show up on your doorstep and kick down the door if necessary. See, your BVCs are the ones who will be there whether you want them to be or not. Back when you were saying "yes" to God, they were saying "yes" to you. If eternity was a neighborhood, your BVCs not only live on your street but they refer to your parents as "mom" and "dad." They don't have to ask to get something to eat or drink out of the refrigerator. They know the password to your wi-fi and your cell phone and will threaten to fight any and everybody who even thinks about bothering you.

Get it?

THESE are the folks you want in your corner when you need a shoulder to cry on or a kick in the butt. And these are the ones who started me on the next part of my journey, the part you are experiencing now.

Remember back in the introduction when I said I didn't want to write this book? Remember when I said I didn't have a choice because, at some point in eternity, I agreed to whatever God decided He had planned for my life? Yeah. I can't count the number of times I've had to remind myself of this over the past year and a half. But apparently, my BVCs were also in on whatever I agreed to because they've been around pushing, pulling, praying, and praising every step of the way. When I get frustrated, tired, depressed, angry, fearful, and a whole host of other emotions, they never judge or berate me. They hear what I say but also listen to what I said.

Puzzled?

You can **hear** someone talking but not **listen** to what they say. If you're a parent, you already know what this is like because our kids tend to do this all…the…time. They **heard** us say, "go to bed," but they didn't actually **listen**.

The difference between the two is simply this: hearing is involuntary while listening is voluntary. Unless your hearing has been impaired in some way, you automatically

hear any noise that passes by your ears. However, to listen requires a conscious effort to make meaning of the noise you heard. My BVCs know how to both hear and listen.
YOUR BVCs need to know how to both hear and listen.

This is important because the people you need to encourage you when you can't encourage yourself must be able to read between the lines. Had the Outer Circle Folks been around on the days when I was falling apart, they would have simply left me alone because who really wants to be around someone who cries all the time? But my BVCs knew what my tears meant. I just didn't have the words to articulate what I needed. That's why they had to listen to my cries, not just hear them.
In Psalm 130, we encounter someone who is experiencing some major trouble and is need of help. Verses 1-2 say:
From the depths of despair, O Lord, I call for your help.
*Hear my cry, O Lord, **pay attention** to my prayer.*

That **pay attention** part is the same as saying "Lord, I don't just need you to hear me. I need you to listen to me." Your BVCs aren't God, but He can use them to do His work on earth, and one of those jobs is listening to you.
So, let me tell you about my BVCs…

For the past few years on January 1, my friend Abby has sponsored a Girlfriends Brunch. (Not her real name. Her real name is much cooler.) An elegant affair, it's a way to start the new year with women of all walks of life over good food, fun, music, prayer, praise, and worship. The first one I attended was so good, I purchased my ticket for 2019 almost as soon as the 2018 brunch was over. Of course, I had no idea what 2018 was going to entail for me so when I realized the brunch was around the corner, I started trying to figure out ways to get out of going.

Since I had purchased my tickets so early, I figured no one would be remiss if I didn't show up. I mean, I bought them before my life fell apart so surely no one really expected me to come!

Abby did.

Five days before January 1 on December 28, Abby sent me a message asking if I was still planning on attending. I remember looking at the message and thinking, "nope." I closed my phone and went on about my day. Incidentally, December 28, isn't just three days after Christmas, it's also three days after my birthday (yes, I'm a Christmas baby) and Christmas 2018 was the worst birthday yet (except for the one where I had to send my daughter to live with my parents. You'll have to wait on the next book to hear about all of that). The **last** thing I wanted to do was think about being at the brunch. At the previous one, I was standing tall (well, tallish,

I'm only 4ft 11inches) wearing a cute dress and cute shoes. This year, I was going to be seated in a wheelchair missing a significant portion of my legs with a blanket across my lap so no one would notice. Wasn't exactly my idea of a great way to start my year. But because God truly does work in mysterious ways, about 30 minutes after receiving the message, and deciding I wasn't going, my daughter comes downstairs and says,

"Aren't you supposed to be going to some brunch thing in a few days?"

Seriously?

I looked at her and feigned ignorance.

"What brunch thing?" How did she even remember that I went last year? She shrugged.

"I don't know. Didn't you go to some brunch thing around this time last year?

Really Lord?

I shrugged my shoulders too.

"Oh. Right. That was on January 1st. I'm not going this year."

"Why not?" My daughter walked into the kitchen and started opening cabinets and drawers looking for something to eat. I rolled my eyes at her question.

"Because I'm not ready," I said and shot her a look that cautioned her to leave the subject alone. To know my daughter means knowing she surely wasn't going to do that. "What aren't you ready for? You had fun last year. I remember you talking about it. You need to go."

So, let me pause for a moment right here and explain a little something about my now 22-year old child. She and I are connected. I can read her like a book and sadly, she can do the same for me. All she has to do is walk in a room where I happen to be, and immediately she knows how I'm feeling. I never have to say a word. You wanna know who else she's connected to?

God.

Been that way since she was a baby. When she was only a few weeks old, my mother was holding her when she started to smile and laugh, and it wasn't one of those baby laughs either. She giggled. At two weeks. I don't know about you, but I wasn't aware that babies could giggle that early, but there she was doing it. That would only be the beginning. I learned quickly that God had her ear.

When she was around four, I was going through a very tough period in my life. It was filled with confusion, depression, and despair and I was trying my best to be the mother I needed to be. I thought I was doing a pretty good job keeping it all together, but the day she sat in her car seat and said that God wanted to know why I wasn't listening to Him I knew I was in trouble.

Back to my story…

"I'm not ready I said." My daughter wasn't paying me a bit of attention as she continued her search for lunch.

"And **I** said you need to go. You'll have fun and besides you need to get out of the house more."

You ever look at your child and wonder where she came from, and then you realize she's you? I'm not going to say that my child is pushy. I'll just say she's persistent. Like her mother.

"Who asked you? Last time I checked I was the mother in this relationship." At this point, she stopped and looked at me with a smirk.

"Yeah you are, and you raised me so…"

Sometimes I can't stand my own child. *insert eye roll here* I doubled down.

"For the last time, I'm not going. Besides, I won't have anyone to take me." What'd I say that for?

"What do you mean? I'll take you. I don't have anything to do that morning and Mr. CJ can pick you up. Problem solved. Now what do you need to wear?" She gave me a broad smile that said, "I said what I said and I'm not going to say it again."

Still not willing to admit defeat, I countered with, "You don't even know what he has to do that day," assuming he would have something to do because my husband, as a pastor, always has **something** to do.

"Hey Mr. CJ," my daughter said enthusiastically on the phone. "Mom has to go to a brunch on January first. I'm going to bring her. Can you pick her up?" My daughter had called in the reinforcements.

Well played kid. Well played.

"Okay cool. Thank you!" She got off the phone and gave me "The Smile of Victory."

"He said he would pick you up so you're going. You're welcome!"

What do you do when you've been successfully handled by your own child? You respond to Abby's message and say, "I'll be there!"

If you haven't figure it out yet, my daughter is a permanent member of the BVC. She is one of my biggest cheerleaders and is quick to remind me **who** I am and **whose** I am if I ever make the mistake and forget. When I was in the hospital and the doctors said I only had a 50/50 chance of making it, she was the first person to shrug it off and say, "you don't know my mother." My heart attack happened while she was home on Spring Break, and she was getting ready to head into mid-terms as soon as she went back. While she was home, she emailed all her professors to let them know what was going on so when she showed up to take her exams a week later, they were understandably confused. One of her professors asked if I was still in the hospital and she told him I was. "Well what are you doing here?" Her response was a perfect example of my daughter's belief in me.

"I need to take my mid-terms. My mom is going to be fine because, well, she's my mom and she's a fighter so I'm not worried. Besides, even if she were to die, she'd somehow find out I missed my mid-terms and haunt me for the rest of my life. Have you ever met my mother? I promise you that's not something I want."

I have the best kid ever.

January 1 finally arrived, and I prepared for the brunch. The brunch colors are purple, so I had her look for the purple dress I wore the previous year, but she couldn't find it. Since I'd been in the hospital, many of my clothes were no longer where I knew them to be thanks to my mother, who went through the house downsizing closets, and my husband who was busy organizing what was left. The only dress she could find was a bright red cocktail dress with ruffles on the sleeves. I immediately regretted agreeing to go. I wanted my purple dress and it was nowhere to be found.

Initiate attitude in 3..2..1..

My daughter, sensing my irritation, piped up and said, "So you're not wearing purple. You're a Delta so no one is going to be surprised that you're wearing red!"
(For those of you who are unfamiliar with this reference, I am a proud member of Delta Sigma Theta Sorority, Incorporated and our colors are Crimson and Cream. I have more red than any one human being should ever be allowed to have. And I'm glad about it)

I scowled. I was already anxious because I was going to stand out just by being in a wheelchair never mind being an amputee, but my daughter was unwavering in her support. She gathered my dress and helped me do my face. She grabbed my shawl, set-up the ramp outside the door, and pushed me to the car.

When we arrived, she rolled me to the door of the event hall and made sure I found my table. Abby had made sure I was at a table at the very front of the room with some of the women who were on program. I figured she had me there because it was the easiest table to get to since I was in a wheelchair. I thought the decision was very thoughtful. I didn't want to be in the way. My daughter kissed me on the forehead and told me to have fun as she smiled, waved, and headed back to the car.

The brunch was amazing as usual. Abby made sure someone fixed my plate and brought me a mimosa (What's a brunch without mimosas??) while I took pictures with some of the women I knew. My anxiety ceased when I realized that no one was staring or treating me any differently than they always had. The music and ministry were exactly what I needed. For the first time in months, I began to feel more than half-way normal.

As the brunch was winding down, Abby began to speak about why she decided to start having the Girlfriends Brunch, to have a place and time when like-minded women could come together for fun, inspiration, and fellowship. It was at that moment that I felt a flutter in my stomach. You know, that feeling you get when something exciting is getting ready to happen? As she continued to speak, she begins talking about an award that she decided she wanted to give annually to a woman who had been through many challenges but was an example of both perseverance and God's grace. A woman who was an example of what it means to trust God despite all that she had been through. Then she says,
"I don't know if you've been following her story on Facebook, but of you have you already know that what I've been saying is true. So today, I would like to present this year's Standing Ovation Award to my sister, Dr. Chantrise Sims Holliman."

The room erupted in applause and everyone stood up.
I cried immediately.

Abby went on to say that January 1 was just the beginning of what God had planned for me. She declared that God was going to blow my mind; that doors would open that had previously been shut; that opportunities to share my story would be presented to me; that I would travel the world and proclaim God's glory through my testimony. That blessings upon blessings were going to come my way. The chorus of "amen" that accompanied each declaration humbled me. I held on to every word, thankful.

When my husband came to pick me up, he was greeted with "hellos" and "hugs. Abby and I aren't just friends, we're members of the same sorority as well as the same church denomination and both she and my husband are in ministry. In fact, the brunch was full of women who knew me because they knew him first through the church. He came to the table and saw my award and smiled.
"Oh. So, what's this?" I began to cry again.
"They gave me a Standing Ovation Award" was all I could get out. He rubbed my back and said,
"Well, you deserve it."

You've probably noticed that I haven't talked about my husband much. I assure you, it's not because I don't have plenty to talk about. He's amazing and if you know even a smidgen of his story then you know "amazing" isn't an exaggeration. He's also the president of the BVC, right up there with my parents who are the founders and my two best friends who are co-VPs. When it comes to encouragement, he doesn't always know what to say but he always knows how to say whatever he says.

When I was in the hospital for the fourth and final time getting my left leg amputated below the knee, he came to visit as he did just about every day. I was having a rough time and was pretty much over everything. He sat down in the chair by my bed. He didn't say much for a while but instead was just present. I think we often overlook how significant the ministry of just being present is. Sometimes folks don't need to hear you say a word. All they really need is for you to be there. That's it. So, my husband was just being when he looked at me and said,

"You are such an amazing woman and I am peacock proud to be your husband."

Had I been standing up I would've collapsed into a sobbing pile of goo. I didn't realize how much I needed to hear that until he said it, but evidently, he knew what I needed to hear. Why?

Because BVCs are good at listening.

Prior to my heart attack and my amputations, I was very self- conscious about my appearance among other things. While I would be considered attractive by many societal standards, I almost never felt like I was pretty enough.

Or small enough.

Or smart enough.

Or qualified enough.

There was always someone prettier, taller, smarter, or qualifiedier than I was (yes, I know that's not a word but just flow with me)

I've battled low self-esteem most of my life, for a variety of reasons, and becoming an amputee didn't make it any better. In the early months I found myself unconsciously preparing myself for rejection from my friends, my family, strangers even, and most of all, my husband. No. He has never not once given me any indication that he would ever leave me and no he has never given me any indication that he didn't take our wedding vows seriously. Everything I was worried about had been conjured up by me in my head. My thoughts had taken over.

(Refer back to Chapter 3).

This one statement meant everything to me. He still thought I was amazing and was still proud to be married to me, even without my legs. For me, it didn't get more encouraging than that.

Proverbs 12: 25 says:

Worry weighs a person down; an encouraging word cheers a person up. (NLT)

And Ecclesiastes 4:9-10 says:

Two people are better off than one, for they can help each other succeed.

If one person falls, the other can reach out and help. But someone who falls alone is in real trouble. (NLT)

Your BVCs are the ones who help lift the burdens off your life. They come around and speak words to help cheer you up. That's their job, their purpose, one of the reasons why they continue to **be** in your life. They pick you up when you fall but you also return the favor when they are in need. Being a BVC isn't one sided. It's reciprocal. You might not be able to be there while you are in need, but you should never forget about who was there when you were.

So, if you don't get anything else out of this chapter, remember this: check your circle. Not everyone should have access to you, especially when you're in your darkest places of struggle. Only the ones who have proven to be faithful, prayerful, consistent, and sincere should be allowed in.

THINK ON THESE THINGS…

Get you some folks who hear you talking but also listen to what you say.

- Reevaluate your circle and kick some people out so you can make room for the type of friends you need. Your BVCs aren't God, but He can use them to do His work on earth, and one of those jobs is listening to you.
- The people you need to encourage you when you can't encourage yourself must be able to read between the lines.
- Being a BVC isn't one sided. It's reciprocal. You might not be able to be there while you are in need, but you should never forget about who was there when you were

Psalm 130 1-2: *From the depths of despair, O Lord, I call for your help.*
Hear my cry, O Lord, ***pay attention*** *to my prayer.*
Proverbs 12:25: *Worry weighs a person down; an encouraging word cheers a person up.* (NLT)
Ecclesiastes 4:9-10: *Two people are better off than one, for they can help each other succeed.*
If one person falls, the other can reach out and help. But someone who falls alone is in real trouble. (NLT)

SISTER STORIES

ENCOURAGEMENT

Waiting on the Wonder-Kid

Judges 13:2-25; 14:1-9; 16:17

Manny sat looking at his computer, frustrated. He sighed loudly. His wife, Hazel, sat on the sofa scrolling through the Amazon app on her phone.

"Babe, do you think this dresser will fit in the baby's room," she asked. Manny mumbled something incoherent to himself.

"Babe. Do you think this dresser will fit in the baby's room?" she asked again. Manny leaned so far back in his chair that Hazel thought he was going to flip over backwards. He clasped his hands behind his head, looked up at the ceiling, and sighed heavily. Hazel shifted herself on the sofa so she could look at her husband. She raised her voice.

"Babe! Helllllloooo?" Manny closed his eyes and rocked back and forth slightly. Finally, Hazel got up from the sofa and stood next to him with her arms folded.

"So, are you ignoring me on purpose or what?" Startled, Manny nearly fell out of the chair.

"What? Huh? Ignore you? What are you talking about?"

"I've been talking to you for the past five minutes Manny and you haven't responded to any of my questions." Manny looked perplexed.

"What questions Hazel?" It was now her turn to sigh loudly.

"Never mind," she mumbled. As she began to walk away, Manny grabbed her hand, pulled her into his lap, and wrapped his arms around her body.

"I'm sorry Puddin'," he said, pressing the side of his face into Hazel's arm. She looked down at him out of the corner of her eye with a look of irritation and sighed loudly. He looked up at her with the best puppy eyes he could muster.

"I luuuuuub you." Hazel rolled her eyes and laughed. It always amazed her how she and Manny had been married for all these years and he still knew how to make her smile. Hazel began to stand up from his lap.

"Uh-huh," she quipped with a playful lilt in her voice. He held her more tightly and buried his face in her side.

"I know you wanna leave me! But I refuse to let you go!" Hazel started laughing out loud.

"Manny quit!" He continued singing.

"If I have to beg and plead for your sympathy, I don't mind 'cause you mean that much to me!" Hazel continued laughing as he stood up, held her hand, and got down on his knees.

"Ain't too proud to beeeggg, sweet darlin! Please don't leave me girl, don't you go!" Hazel tried to pull away, but Manny continued holding her hand while on his knees. As she attempted to walk away, he grabbed her arm and pressed it to his cheek. He sang louder.

"Ain't too proud to pleeeeaaad, baby, baby! Please don't leave me girl don't you go!" By this time Hazel was in full out hysterics. She laughed loudly again.

"MANNY! Stop it!" Finally, he let go of her hand and arm and laughed as he stood up.

"You know you love me," he said as he leaned over and kissed her on the cheek enthusiastically. Hazel caught her breath and flopped back down on the sofa.

"I do but you get on my nerves!" Hazel giggled as she wiped away the tears that had welled up in her eyes from laughing.

"Something is so very wrong with you!" Manny sat down next to her and leaned back on the sofa.

"Welp, you knew that before you married me so who's fault is that?" Hazel leaned against his arm. He moved it out of the way so she could lean against his chest. He kissed her on the forehead.

"Now, what were you trying to ask me?"

"I was asking you if you thought the dresser I'd found would fit in the baby's room and you were so busy sighing and ignoring me you didn't hear my question. What's wrong?" Manny rubbed her arm as he held her close and sighed once again.

"You know how I won those tickets to the Dolphins game next Sunday?" Hazel nodded.

"Well, none of the guys can go with me." Manny and his friends were lifelong fans of the Miami Dolphins so when he won tickets to watch a game from one of the owner's suites, he began making plans for all six of them to attend. Unfortunately, none of them were available. Hazel smirked, "Well you could always take your wife and her girlfriends." Manny looked down at the top of her head.
"Oh, so I can spend the entire game listening to y'all root for The Cowboys? Anyway…" Hazel sat up and shrugged her shoulders.
"Hey, it's not MY fault you chose to support a team that hasn't made the playoffs since 2000." Manny looked at his wife and rolled his eyes.

Hazel was born and raised in Dallas, while Manny was born and raised in Miami. The rivalry between their two teams is what brought them together when they were in college. Manny's frat brother was hosting a watch party to which Hazel and her sorority sisters were invited. Neither of their teams were playing but they each wore their team's jersey. It was an issue the minute she walked through the door.

Manny approached her and made a comment about her team. She countered with a comment about his team and on it went for the rest of the evening. Before the night was over,

Manny and Hazel found themselves on the balcony of the apartment arguing over stats, players, and all things football. Manny was impressed by her in depth knowledge of the game and Hazel was impressed that he didn't try to dismiss her because she was a girl.

After that meeting, they would see each other on campus and even had a few courses together. This allowed them to get to know each other better and it wasn't long before they were the "it" couple. Manny proposed to Hazel at the beginning of their Junior year and at age 20, they decided to get married. Their parents weren't too keen on the idea but supported their children's decision. Fifteen years later, they were still together and just as in love as they were in school. The only thing missing was a child. Unfortunately, during their 15 years of marriage, they had been unable to conceive. But that was all getting ready to change.

"You're gonna stop bad mouthing my team," Manny said as he stood up from the sofa. Hazel turned sideways on the sofa and grabbed her phone.

"Just as soon as your team does something worthy of me NOT bad mouthing them." Manny chuckled and walked back to the chair in front of his computer.

"Now what dresser are you talking about?" He logged on to his computer.

"I emailed you the link," Hazel said. Manny opened the link Hazel had sent.

"Uh, honey? Why are there red elephants all over this dresser?" Hazel shifted her position so she could look over the sofa and see her husband and smiled.

"Isn't it cute?" she asked enthusiastically.

"Hazel, I'm not putting a dresser covered in red elephants in our son's room."

"Why not," Hazel inquired. "Elephants are very masculine and red is the color of power!" Manny looked back at her and smirked.

"Hazel, I'm not putting red elephants in our son's room." Hazel cocked her head to the side and smirked back.

"What if they were purple and gold elephants?"

Manny chuckled. "We already have too many elephants in the house, Hazel." She turned back to her phone on the sofa.

"Manny, there is no such thing as having too many elephants."

"Of course, you'd say that. Find another dresser Hazel." She looked over her shoulder and stuck her tongue out.

"Anyway...," she responded. "So, what are you going to do about the game? Why aren't the guys available?" Manny began scrolling through the Amazon site.

"Apparently they're all going to a Father-Son event after church and won't be available." Hazel could hear the disappointment in her husband's voice.
"Well next year you'll be able to go too" she smiled. Manny furrowed his brow and mumbled.
"I guess."
"Manny," Hazel said softly, "we really are going to have a baby boy." Manny sighed.
"I know. I know." He responded to appease his wife, but he really wasn't sure. Hazel stood up from the sofa and walked back over to where Manny was seated. She leaned against the desk and looked at him.
"Why is it so hard for you to believe what Pastor Angelo said to me?" Manny looked at his wife.
"First of all, I wasn't there when he said it, so I don't know WHAT he said. Two, we've been trying to have a baby for years and nothing has worked. C, refer back to the first."

For Manny, this was a sensitive issue. They had been praying nearly their entire marriage for a child and for years they were hopeful, believing God would hear their prayers and answer affirmatively. After 10 years of trying, and trusting, and waiting, they got discouraged, convinced that having a child just wasn't in God's plan. Then, out of the blue, about a month prior, Hazel went to a mid-week revival at church. Manny had to work late, or he would've been there, and he wished he had been. That night their Pastor, Pastor Angelo, called Hazel out from the congregation and asked her to come to the altar. He told her that God had woken him up out of a sound sleep and told him that she was going to have a baby boy within a year. Hazel came home and shared with Manny what Pastor Angelo had said. She was so overcome with joy that she wept during the entire conversation. All Manny could do was hold her. He didn't want to dampen her joy. Afterall, this was the answer to their prayers, but Manny was skeptical. He didn't so much have an issue with **what** was said. He had an issue with who it was coming from. Why would God just tell Pastor Angelo and not the people who had been praying?

Hazel folded her arms. "So, we're back to this again?" Manny went back to looking at his computer.

"Hazel, I'm not saying he **didn't** say it I just...," his voice trailed off.

"Do you trust me," Hazel asked. Manny smirked. Hazel asked again.

"Do you trust me?" Manny tried to avoid making his next statement but the mischievousness in him wouldn't allow it.

"Oh, so we're channeling *Aladdin,* are we? If you're Aladdin does that make me Jasmine, cuz if it does, I'm not wearing harem pants." Manny looked up with a smile but was met with Hazel's disapproving scowl. He sighed softly.

"Yes Hazel. You know I trust you." Hazel's face softened.

"Then believe what I heard and believe what he said." She touched Manny's hand and looked at him lovingly. Then she said softly,

"Clearly, if you can believe that the Dolphins are going to actually make the playoffs this year you can believe we're going to have a baby. I mean which is the bigger miracle?" Manny hung his head and chuckled as she walked to the kitchen smiling.

****

"Hello?" Hazel answered the phone.

"Hey there Pastor Angelo! How are you?"

"I'm excellent Sister Hazel. You and Manny getting that baby room together?" Hazel smiled.

"We've been looking at furniture. I found the cutest dresser with red elephants on it, but Manny said his son wasn't going to sleep in a room with red elephants all over his dresser." Pastor Angelo laughed heartily.

"Well do you blame him?"

Hazel responded, "I told him we could paint them purple and gold! He still said 'no.'"

"I'm gonna have to agree with my Frat on this one," Pastor Angelo laughed. Hazel pouted.

"I'm gonna get my elephants in that room somehow."

"Of that I have no doubt," Pastor Angelo chuckled. "Now, are you taking care of yourself? Eating right? No alcohol, no fatty foods? Lots of water and fruits and veggies? You're carrying greatness in you Hazel and we need to make sure you're healthy so he can be healthy."

"I'm doing all of that Pastor Angelo. Now if I could just get Manny not to be so discouraged."

"Discouraged?" asked Pastor Angelo.

"Yup," said Hazel. "I've been trying to keep him encouraged but it's been difficult. He wants to believe that this baby is going to come but he's still doubtful."

"I understand," said Pastor Angelo. "Y'all have been waiting a long time for this. It's hard to believe when you've been praying so long for something and it just doesn't seem like God is listening." Hazel nodded her head.

"That's it exactly. Do you think you could talk to him? Tell him what you told me?"

"Funny you would ask that since that's actually the reason why I called. I'm leaving the church right now and wanted to stop by and holla at my frat." Hazel smiled.

"Yes!" she yelled. "Manny's in his office. I'll tell him you're stopping by."

"I'll be there in 10 minutes. See you soon." Hazel hung up the phone and ran to Manny's office.

"Manny!"

"Mmhmm…" Manny responded as he was engrossed in a document on his computer.

"Manny! Pastor Angelo is on his way over." Manny looked up.

"For what?"

"He said he was leaving the church and wanted to stop by and holla at his frat." Hazel rolled her eyes.

"Cool," Manny said. "I can tell him about your plot to 'elephantize' the baby's room."

"I already told him, and he agrees with you. Figures." Hazel rolled her eyes again. She exited the room and went to the kitchen to get some water. A few minutes later the doorbell rang.

"Manny!" Hazel yelled. "Pastor Frat is at the door!" Manny slowly jogged from his office to the door and opened it.

"What's up Pastor?" Manny gave him the compulsory fraternity handshake. Pastor Angelo responded as he walked through the door.

"Nothin' much. What's going on with you?

"Man, trying to keep Hazel from taking over this baby's room." Manny shut the door behind him.

"I heard! Red elephants, huh?" Pastor Angelo chuckled. Manny hung his head and shook it.

"I'm gonna need your prayers on this one Reverend." The two men walked into the living room where Hazel was waiting. She stood up when they entered.

"Hey Pastor Angelo." Hazel approached and gave him a hug.

"Hey Sis," he responded. "How you doin'?"

"I'm fine, "she said, "but your BOY over here keeps bothering me." Hazel tossed her head sideways in Manny's direction.

"I'm bothering YOU? Oh, so we're just gonna lie in front of the pastor, huh?" Manny put his hand on Pastor Angelo's shoulder. "Don't listen to her. She's the one bothering me!" Angelo laughed.

"Now I know my sweet sister couldn't POSSIBLY be bothering you!" Manny rolled his eyes

"Don't let that face fool you, Reverend." Manny sat down next to Hazel on the sofa and kissed her on the cheek.

"So, I heard you wanted to stop by. What's up?" Manny put his arm around Hazel's shoulder.
"Nothing much. Just wanted to see how you were doing." Pastor Angelo sat down on the loveseat facing them.
"We're doing well," Manny responded.
"Not 'you' plural; 'You' singular. How are YOU doing Manny?" Manny looked puzzled.
"I'm good Reverend. I'm good." Pastor Angelo put his elbows on his knees and leaned forward.
"So, you ready for your son to arrive." Manny sighed
"Ahh. So that's what this is all about. Okay, listen." Manny removed his arm from around Hazel's shoulder, sat up, and clapped his hands together.
"Let me make myself clear. I want Hazel and I to have a baby. I'm **excited** about Hazel and I having a baby one day…" Hazel interrupted.
"Not one day Manny, soon." Manny sighed, looked at his wife and then back at Pastor Angelo.
"This has been a daily conversation since you told her we were having a child and I'm about tired of it. Look, why would God tell you that we were going to have a baby and not tell either one of us?" Pastor Angelo leaned back on the sofa.
"He did tell you." Manny leaned forward.
"Nah man. You said He told YOU. He didn't tell us."

"Correct. He did tell me, and I told Hazel who then told you." Manny began to get agitated.

"Which means He didn't tell US! Why would He tell a stranger and not tell us? Sorry. You're our pastor and my frat and all but nah, I'm not buying." Manny could feel Hazel tense up next to him. He went to put his hand on her knee when she got up suddenly.

"Hazel where are you going?" Without saying a word, she walked out of the room. Manny sighed and looked back at Pastor Angelo.

"Look. I know you meant well but this whole thing is causing issues." Pastor Angelo looked back at Manny.

"Causing issues with who? Hazel believes. Why don't you?" Manny began to speak but was interrupted.

"Look Manny, I don't just say whatever in my pulpit. If God didn't give it to me, I'm not saying in it. Point blank period. You know that. When God gave me the vision, the first thing I said was 'So, you're gonna tell them, right?' The response I got was 'No. You are.' Man, I was like 'are You sure God? I mean You can tell them Yourself.' You know what I got back? 'I could, but they can't hear me anymore." Pastor Angelo got quiet. Manny began to speak again.

"It's just been so long, and we've prayed and prayed and nothing." He sighed. "Like I've been saying, I want us to have a child I just don't know…" His voice trailed off. "I guess we haven't been praying like we used to. It's just hard, man. It's just hard." At that moment, Hazel quietly returned into the room and stood by the sofa. It was clear she had been crying.
"Hazel, what's wrong?" Manny stood up and started to approach her when she put up her hand to say "stop."
"No Manny. Stay right there. I need you to sit right there." Tears continued to stream down her face.
"I heard what Pastor Angelo said, that God told him to tell us about our baby boy because we stopped listening to Him. That's true. We haven't been praying. We haven't been studying. We even stopped asking. Since Pastor Angelo told us we were having a son, I've prayed more than I've prayed in months. I've believed more than I've believed in months. I've trusted more than I've trusted in months! And now…" Hazel reached into her pocket and pulled out an item wrapped in a paper towel. She sat down next to him, carefully unwrapped it, and placed it in Manny's hand.
"And now…," she sniffled, "I know He heard us." Manny looked at what Hazel gave him. On the thin plastic stick, in bold black lettering, was a single word: Pregnant.

Manny sat perfectly still, staring at the pregnancy test before looking up into the face of his wife.

"Pregnant?" he asked. Hazel shook her head and smiled as the tears flowed down her cheeks.

"Pregnant." She said softly.

Manny looked at Pastor Angelo who had his eyes closed and his head hung down, with his elbows on his knees and his hands clasped in front of him.

"Pastor Angelo. Frat. Bruh!" Manny jumped up, grabbed Pastor Angelo by the hand, and pulled him up.

"We're pregnant!" he shouted.

"Well, she's pregnant! I mean…we're having a baby!" He continued to shake Pastor Angelo's hand vigorously. Manny put one hand on his forehead. Pastor Angelo laughed.

"Yes. Yes, you are. Congratulations to you both!" Hazel continued to sit on the sofa overcome by tears. Finally, she grabbed a tissue and wiped her eyes. Laughing, she said, "See Manny. I TOLD you! I guess if God can work out this miracle, He can work one out for your Dolphins too."

Manny laughed. "See what I mean Frat. Who's really bothering who?" Pastor Angelo laughed also.

"Look man. I don't know how to thank you. Listen, let me, us, take you to dinner or at least fix you a meal!" Pastor Angelo shook his head.

"No sir. I don't need anything to eat. I'm good. The only thing I want you to do for me is praise God. All of the glory belongs to Him." Pastor Angelo pointed toward the ceiling.

"He deserves it, not me."

Hazel came over and hugged him.

"Thank you. Thank you. Thank you! Now, about these red elephants I want…"

Chapter 5

All I Do Is Win

San Antonio, Texas.
Home to the River Walk, The Alamo, and the five-time NBA Championship winning San Antonio Spurs.

It was also the location of the 2019 Amputee Coalition Conference that I really didn't want to go to. By the time of the conference, I had been told by more than one professional that the nerve damage in my legs was so severe that I probably would never walk again. So, being at a conference with a bunch of people walking and running with their protheses was not my idea of a good time. The thought was depressing and just brought me back to the pain of hearing the term "nerve damage" for the first time.

My first encounter with my PT guy Craig was almost my last.

I was referred to him by my prosthetist back in October 2018 when I was told that all I needed was some intense physical therapy to strengthen my legs. My in-home physical therapist decided that after working with me for four weeks, she had done all she could so going to see Craig was the next step.

When I arrived at his office, I was excited to get going. I figured if I worked hard enough, I might be walking or maybe even running by October 2019. Hard work didn't scare me. Prior to my heart attack I would run 5 miles every morning at 5:00 and had gotten myself down to a 10-minute mile. It was the challenge that came with pushing myself that I liked. When I got to Craig's, I was ready to push again.

His first task was to do an evaluation of my physical ability so he could come up with an appropriate plan of action. He asked a few questions and then led me through a few leg exercises. When I got back in my chair, I sat next to his desk while he typed his notes. I watched him for a few minutes and then he said five words that made me hate him almost immediately.

"You're presenting like a paraplegic."

I looked at him dumbfounded. Of all the things he could've said…

"What do you mean I'm presenting as a paraplegic?" He furrowed his brow.

"Well, your legs are weak, far weaker than they should be even with the weeks you spent in the hospital."

"They told me that my legs had atrophied while I was in the hospital the first time," I explained, "but all I needed was physical therapy." Craig looked at the concern in my face and continued.

"So, did a neurologist ever come and see you, you know, to check out your legs?"

"Not for my legs, no, "I told him. "My cognitive ability, yes, but not my legs." He frowned again.

"We need to get you to a neurologist so we can see how badly the nerves in your legs have been damaged. Nerves **can** repair themselves, but they only grow about an inch a month and there's no guarantee that they will."

Yup. Wasn't ever going back to see Craig again.

Ever.

Clearly, he didn't know what he was talking about and how dare he tell me I was presenting as a paraplegic on my first day? Where was the sensitivity? Where was the compassion? It was there (as I found out after I decided to keep working with him) but it was always going to be wrapped in the truth.

"I'm never going to lie to you or say things just to make you feel better. I am always going to be honest with you with regards to your progress and the challenges you are facing. I hate when I'm the first person to tell a patient something she should've already known. Now let's see if we can find you a neurologist."

It took almost four months before I was able to see the neurologist, and he confirmed exactly what Craig had said. The nerve damage in my legs was severe. When he used the nerve hammer on my arms, they responded accordingly. When he used it to hit my knee, nothing happened. If the nerves were working correctly, my leg would have extended outward. I barely even felt it.

Craig continued to work with me, trying every therapy and technique he could think of to help my legs regain some movement. I worked hard but my progress was minimal so he began suggesting things I could do to regain some of my independence, like getting my car fitted for hand controls so I could drive again and purchasing a light weight wheelchair that I could put in and out of the car by myself. He was supportive and funny but wouldn't allow my mother or my surrogate mother to help me with my wheelchair.

"What if she falls trying to get in and out of the car?" they'd ask.

"She'll figure out how to either a) get back in the car or b) get into her chair. Either way, she'll learn a really important lesson."

Yup. Gotta love my PT guy Craig.

But it was that kind of tough love that didn't make me too upset when a few weeks before the Amputee Coalition Conference, he sent me home with a packet full of upper body exercises and told me to come back and see him when I regained some significant movement in my legs. By this time, I was a pro at driving with my hand controls and getting the wheelchair in and out of the car by myself and I had only had one accident. (*Note to self: Never again try to exit your house without the ramp unless you want to face plant on the concrete.*

Thankfully, all I ended up with was a skinned knee and a slightly bruised ego. But I figured out how to get back in my chair just like Craig said I would.)

Back to San Antonio…

When we arrived in Texas, my first encounter with a San Antonian was a man waiting for a taxi with is friend outside the airport. In the early months, I used to hate for people to see my residual limbs (that's the technical term for my legs post amputation) but I don't know if you know this, Atlanta, in the summer, is hot. San Antonio in the summer is hotter and the last thing I wanted to do was have anything covering up my legs. As they were talking, the first man turned in my direction, saw me, turned up his nose, shook his head and turned around so he could no longer see me.
Oh yes. This trip was **definitely** going to be fun! *Insert sarcasm here*

At the hotel, things didn't get any better. My mother had requested a handicap accessible room when she registered for the conference back in March but when we arrived, we were told that the conference had taken all the rooms and distributed them to the people they felt needed them most. I was okay with not having a special room since I had traveled enough earlier in the year to know that I could do what I needed to do in a room that wasn't accessible. "Either you make a way, or you make a way" was my motto. The world is not made for people who are differently abled, so I learned very quickly how to adjust to make things work for me. I was very thankful I could.

No biggie.

My mother on the other hand was hearing none of that. It didn't matter that we were in a hotel with only 20 handicap accessible rooms at a conference where literally everyone could've used a handicap accessible room. She was upset that she put her request in early and no one told her that it might not be honored. My mother is the Queen of Customer service and I assure you being on the receiving end of her wrath is not a pleasant place to be.

Nevertheless, we persisted.

As we were heading to the elevator to our room, I noticed a sign that listed all the sessions for the day. I really didn't' plan on attending any sessions at all because, as I suspected, most of them were either a) for people who used prostheses or b) weren't topics I was interested in. But there was one session for people who didn't use prostheses that started in about an hour. I decided that if I was going to attend one session, that was going to be it. My intention was to enjoy being in a hotel room where I could use the bathroom and take a shower and work on this book.

When we got to the session, the first thing I noticed was I was the only female amputee in the room. The other women there were the physical therapist presenting and two women who were also physical therapists. Even though I chose the session, I was full of attitude. The presenter started by saying that the information she was going to share came from the Amputee Coalition website and I thought, "well I could've stayed in the room and looked the information up myself."

Fold arms, frown, roll eyes

Her name was Marjorie and she was a physical therapist who was trained to work specifically with amputees. She continued by saying her session was more about getting people who didn't use prostheses to share the tips or tricks they used in daily life than it was about **her** sharing anything. But, as I looked around the room, I noticed that everyone had at least one prosthetic device, except me.

Fold arms, frown, and roll eyes harder

After she shared a few statistics she asked,

"What are some reasons why some people choose not to get prostheses?" A few people responded and then I raised my hand and said, "because you're told you can't get them."

Marjorie looked at me puzzled and said, "Who told you that?"

"My physical therapist and the neurologist I went to see. I have severe nerve damage in my legs, so I was told that as a result I'll probably never get prostheses." Marjorie frowned.

"Wow. So, you've never had any? Never even tried?"

I shook my head, "nope." By this time Marjorie was frowning **and** looking puzzled.

"I'm going to talk to you after this session is over."

When it ended, she smiled at me and asked my name then sat on the floor in front of me.

"Now, tell me again why you've never been fitted for prostheses. Is it okay of I examine your residual limb?" I told her it was, and I proceeded to share with her my journey since learning about the nerve damage. As I was talking, she was lifting my left limb up and down. She asked me to close my eyes and imagine I still had feet and try to point my toes.

"Ah," she exclaimed. "I felt that!" She then asked me about my ability to move my other limb and my range of motion. I told her everything I was able to do, and she began thinking out loud.

"Do you have a prosthetist?" I told her I did but I hadn't seen him since December after delivering the news to him from Craig.

"What's his name?"

"Derek Chang," I said. Immediately Marjorie lit up.

"THAT'S who your prosthetist is?? Derek and I have known each other for almost 20 years! We used to work together. I'm going to call him today and tell him we spoke and that you need some legs!"

By this time, we had left the room because another session was starting, and we were talking in the hallway. Marjorie was positively gleeful.

"Derek should be able to make you a set of legs. I'm going to tell him what kind of legs he needs to make so he can get you fitted.

" I just looked at her amazed. How was it possible that a woman who had only known me for less than an hour was confident that I could have prosthetic limbs? How was she so confident that she was going to contact my prosthetist and tell him exactly what he needed to build?

"Now, where do you live?" Still stunned, I responded.

"Southwest Atlanta, about 20 minutes from the airport." Her smile broadened.

"You're about 30 minutes from me. I work out of Peachtree City. After you get your legs, you can come and work with me. We'll have you walking in no time!" Her enthusiasm was almost frightening.

This couldn't possibly be happening, not after all I had been told. I'm in San Antonio meeting a physical therapist who believes I can walk, decides to call my prosthetist, tells him what he needs to build, and agrees to work with me so I can walk again. I started to cry.

"I don't even know how to explain to you what I'm feeling right now. When I was told I would never be able to get protheses all I could think of was how I'd never be able to go back home to my parents' house, that I'd never be able to walk in the door, or sleep in my bed. Even if I was able to get in the house, I wouldn't be able to move about because the doorways are too narrow. I would go to visit my mom and dad and I'd have to stay in a hotel." The more I cried, the more my mother cried, and the more Marjorie smiled at me gently.

"You were supposed to be in San Antonio, and you were supposed to be in my session. I don't believe in coincidences. We were supposed to meet."

****

When I returned home, I contacted Derek's office to set my appointment. His assistant told me that he was so excited when Marjorie called him, he couldn't wait to see me back in his office. My appointment was set for a week later.

My husband and I arrived at our scheduled time. As we were waiting to be called back to one of the exam rooms, a woman wearing her prostheses wheeled out and began speaking to us.

"Are you here to get prosthetics?" I wasn't sure how to respond since I didn't know if I was going to actually get them or not. My husband responded instead.

"Yes, she is." The woman smiled and began speaking excitedly about her prosthetics and how it took her a little while to learn how to use them but that she was getting better with practice. Then she looked at me and said, "You'll get the hang of it too with practice. You can do it!"

I smiled and nodded and said, "thank you" while my husband answered, "yes, she can!"

When we finally got to see Derek, his enthusiasm was palpable. He told me that he wondered what happened to me after I left his office in December and he was over the moon excited when Marjorie called him. He explained to us what Marjorie had told him and he was already coming up with ideas for my new legs.

My new legs.

MY new legs.

I just liked the way that sounded.

The original plan was for him to simply evaluate me and then schedule an appointment for me to come back to have molds of my legs made. But the plan changed when, after stepping out for a moment, he returned and asked if we

had time that day for him to create the molds.
"Both of my afternoon appointments cancelled so I have time if you have time!" We had the time, but honestly, even if we didn't, we were going to make the time. What man said wasn't possible was becoming a reality. I was floored.
Once he was done creating the mold, Derek said "Okay. Come back in a week and make sure you bring a pair of shoes. What size shoe do you wear?"

What size shoe do I wear?

A month prior, I would've been offended by the question. But on this day, I heard myself say, "I wear a size six."
"Cool. Make sure you bring your favorite shoes with you when you come. A pair of sneakers will work."

A week later, my daughter and I arrived with my favorite red and white, bedazzled, low top Chuck Taylors in hand. Derek's assistant Chris came in with a smile and my daughter handed him my shoes. I was anxious but excited. When Derek walked back in the room carrying my legs, my heart started racing in my chest.
"They're not pretty, but they'll suffice for now. We need to see what works and what doesn't before I make you your permanent set. After you work with Marjorie for about a month, we'll make whatever adjustments need to be made." Derek smiled. "You ready?"

I took a deep breath and shook my head yes.

Derek led me over to set of parallel bars and helped me get my new legs on. My daughter was standing off to the side recording everything on her phone. He told me to grab each of the parallel bars and pull myself up to standing.

One…two…three…

For the first time in over a year,

I stood up straight.

I could feel the vertebrae in my lower back snap, crackle, and pop. I had been in a seated position for so long, it almost felt like they let out a sigh of relief.

At that moment, my husband walked in the door and smiled.

"Look at you!" I smiled back.

Derek showed me what to push and pull to make my knees lock and unlock and we practiced sitting down and standing up. Then he said, "Okay. Take a step." Instinctively, I did.

And it felt marvelous.

Holding on to the parallel bars, I took another step. And then another. And then another.

"Well let me just get out of your way then," Derek quipped.

I got to the end of the bars and turned around and walked back to my chair, turned around, and sat down. I was already tired. The prosthetics were heavy, and they had to be. Because of the nerve damage, Derek had to add additional pieces to provide the stability I needed to support my body weight. But I was so happy I didn't care.

He left me with some instructions, and we took the legs off. I couldn't walk without holding on to the parallel bars, so my husband carried them out of the office for me. My daughter, who had been recording, switched to sending copies of the video to everyone she could think of as well as posting on social media. My husband followed suite and so did I. There was a social media bonanza going on and we were loving every minute of it.

One week later, I found myself in Peachtree City with Marjorie and my surrogate mom, Mama Dee. The evaluation she did was very different than my first one with Craig. She focused on what I could do and then led me to a set of short parallel bars. She sat on the floor in front of me with the same smile and enthusiasm she had when we first met those weeks ago. Mama Dee grabbed her phone and started recording. "Okay! Let's see you stand." I stood up and she said "good!" She had me walk to the end of the parallel bars and turn around.

"Okay. Now, what I want you to do is try to balance without holding on to the parallel bars. I'm right here behind you so you won't fall but I want you to try and find your center of balance and see if you can stand up straight."

We were all amazed when I let go of the parallel bars and stood up straight.

It took me a few wobbles to find my center of gravity, but I did it.

One of the best parts about watching this recording (which I've done dozens of times by now), is watching Marjorie's face as she realizes what I'm doing. The other best part is hearing her say, "Wow. You're balancing and turning your head during your first session! Do you know how hard that is to do? Do you understand it takes most amputees a long time to do what you've already done on your first day? You are on your way!"

****

[3]He will say to them, 'Listen to me, all you men of Israel!

Do not be afraid as you go out to fight your enemies today!

Do not lose heart or panic or tremble before them.

[4]For the Lord your God is going with you!

He will fight for you against your enemies, and He will give you victory!'

Deuteronomy 20: 3-4 (NLT)

Who are your enemies? What does the word "enemy" even mean?

Glad you asked.

According to Dictionary.com, an "enemy" is *a person who feels hatred for, fosters harmful designs against, or engages in antagonistic activities against another; an adversary.* And while everything before the semi-colon is absolutely true, I want you to ignore it and focus on what comes after the semi-colon. An "enemy" is **an adversary**. So, what exactly is an "adversary?"

Well, it depends on which definition you use. One of the definitions of "adversary" is personified to be synonymous with Satan but I don't want to talk about him. Yes, some things that happen in our lives are as a result of 'ol Beelzebub's trickery, but it's the other definition that I want to address. An "adversary" is *a person, group, or* ***force*** *that opposes or attacks; a person, group, or physical or* ***mental power that opposes or attacks****.*

In each of these chapters, I've shared only snippets of my journey. I promise, you don't have time to read the full-length version. And yet, through all of that, the only **physical** adversary I had to fight was myself, and I was doing a pretty good job beating myself up because of the **mental** adversaries I had given power to. I call them **The Four D's**:

Despair

Doubt

Depression

and **Displeasure.**

Individually, these four could've easily done what the heart attack and the amputations didn't. Collectively, they should have. Many people have died either physically, spiritually, emotionally of morally as a result of **one** of The Four D's.

So, when I read the scripture above, I just get happy. Let's look at the part in bold once more:

[4]For the Lord your God is going with you!

He will fight for you against your enemies, and He will give you victory!'

In Chapter 3, I spoke about what it means to overcome, and I gave it the title, "This Doesn't Feel Like Victory" because it doesn't. While we're busy in the overcoming stage, we are still fighting everything that's going on in our heads that's telling us none of it is worth it. We feel like every time we move forward once we get pushed back five. But it doesn't matter what it feels like. The only thing that matters is God is going with us to victory. And not only is He going **with** us, He's fighting **for** us which means He's fighting on our behalf. **AND** if all of that wasn't good enough, He's giving the victory to us.

Giving.

To present voluntarily and without expecting compensation.

He's going **with** us. He's fighting **for** us. He's giving the victory **to** us.

If that doesn't make you smile, shout, hoot, and/or holler, well I just don't know what to say.

While **I** was busy trying to fight The Four D's (there I go trying to be in control again), God had already secured the victory. He'd already fought the fight and won. And when you're busy trying to fight whatever your mental adversaries are, guess what God's doing?

Winning. On your behalf.

You know why?

"…This is what the Lord says: Do not be afraid! Don't be discouraged by [your adversaries], ***for the battle is not yours, but God's****."* 2 Chronicles 20:15 (NLT)

Here's how I heard one person interpret this scripture: The battle is His, so the victory is mine.

Boom.

Victories manifest in a bunch of different ways, both mentally and physically, just like adversaries. My mental victories came when I let go of my need to be in control. They came when I decided to surrender to God's will for my life. They came when I chose to change my mindset to combat my "stinkin' thinkin." My physical victories came when I received my prostheses. They came when I was able to stand, when I was able to walk, and when I was able to balance and all of it after being told that none of it would ever happen.

***But [Jesus] said, "what is impossible for people, is possible with God."* Luke 18:27 (NLT)**

Victories aren't just one-offs you know. Just as sure as we will encounter challenges and obstacles, we can also be assured that victories will follow. How do I know? Well, for a few reasons:

1) John 16:33 says:

"I have told you all this so that you may have peace in me. ***Here on earth you will have many trials and sorrows. But take heart, because I have overcome the world."*** (NLT)

2) And Romans 8:28 says:

And we know that God causes everything to work together for the good of those who love God and are called according to His purpose for them. (NLT)

3) And 1 Corinthians 10:13 says:

No test or temptation that comes your way is beyond the course of what others have had to face. *All you need to remember is that God will never let you down; He'll never let you be pushed past your limit;* ***he'll always be there to help you come through it.*** (MSG)

And finally, lest we slip back into doubt and worry and think that the victory won't ever come, we must choose to believe that every promise God made to us is true because, after all,

God is not a man, so he does not lie. He is not human, so He does not change His mind.

Has He ever spoken and failed to act?

Has He ever promised and not carried it through? Numbers 23:19 (NLT)

And it is so. Amen?

Amen.

THINK ON THESE THINGS…

After every obstacle, a victory awaits..

- What are the mental adversaries you need to overcome?
- God goes **with** us. He fights **for** us. He gives the victory **to** us.
- The battle is His, so the victory is ours.
- Victories aren't just one-offs.. Just as sure as we will encounter challenges and obstacles, we can also be assured that victories will follow.

Deuteronomy 20: 3-4: *[3]He will say to them, 'Listen to me, all you men of Israel!*
Do not be afraid as you go out to fight your enemies today!
Do not lose heart or panic or tremble before them.
[4]For the Lord your God is going with you!
He will fight for you against your enemies, and He will give you victory!' (NLT)

2 Chronicles 20:15: *"…This is what the Lord says: Do not be afraid! Don't be discouraged by [your adversaries], for the battle is not yours, but God's."* (NLT)

Luke 18:27: *But [Jesus] said, "what is impossible for people, is possible with God."* (NLT)

John 16:33: *"I have told you all this so that you may have peace in me. Here on earth you will have many trials and sorrows. But take heart, because I have overcome the world."* (NLT)

Romans 8:28: *And we know that God causes everything to work together for the good of those who love God and are called according to His purpose for them.* (NLT)

1 Corinthians 10:13: *No test or temptation that comes your way is beyond the course of what others have had to face. All you need to remember is that God will never let you down; He'll never let you be pushed past your limit; he'll always be there to help you come through it.* (MSG)

Numbers 23:19: *God is not a man, so he does not lie. He is not human, so He does not change His mind.Has He ever spoken and failed to act?*
Has He ever promised and not carried it through? (NLT)

SISTER STORIES SUCCESS

The Number Seven
Luke 8:1-3

Mary sipped her tea slowly as she watched the wind play tag in what was left of the leaves on the oak tree in her front yard. The sheer size of it meant it kept much of her front porch cool in the summer, but it also meant it wreaked havoc on her gutters in the fall. When she and Bill first came to look at the house all those years ago, it was the tree that drew her in with its long sturdy boughs. They looked like arms welcoming her in. Her husband, however, was less impressed.

"Isn't she beautiful, Bill?" Mary remembered asking.

"Un-huh," Bill responded. "That's a huge tree Mary, with a whole lot of leaves. Who exactly is going to rake all of them?"

Mary barely heard his question. Even then, she remembered being soothed by the gentle rustling sound of the leaves as they were disturbed by the breeze. In fact, it was one of the few things that soothed her at all.

"Mary…" Bill said. She closed her eyes and let the breeze wash over her senses.

"Lovely," she whispered. "Just lovely…" It wasn't until she felt Bill's hand on her elbow that she awoke from her trance. She opened her eyes and found herself looking into his slightly frowning face.

"Are you okay?" Bill asked. "I kept calling your name but you weren't responding. Are you feeling alright?" Mary had lost track of time standing under the old oak and hadn't realized both Bill and the realtor had made their way up the steps of the front porch and into the house. Bill had to come back outside to retrieve her.

"I'm sorry dear," Mary said apologetically. "It's just so peaceful out here. I guess I let myself drift away. I didn't mean to worry you." She patted his hand. "I'm ready to go inside now."

As she started for the house, she sensed Bill's concern. Ever since her father died, she hadn't quiet felt like herself even though they were never very close. Mary's mother passed away when she was young and her father wasn't sure how to raise a grieving little girl. So, he threw himself into his work as a successful entrepreneur and left Mary to her own devices. Everything she learned about being a young woman she learned from either television or the few friends she had at school. This was not to say that she wasn't cared for, at least in the tangible sense. Mary never wanted for anything since her

father made sure she got whatever she asked for, but she considered him to be more "the guy she lived with" than she did "dad." That's why it surprised both her and Bill when she got the news of her father's death and almost immediately went into a depression.

Her father had lived a good long life and his homegoing was well attended. Most of those who were present were business associates or former clients. Mary was the only family member there other than Bill since all her father's siblings and other relatives had died before him and she was an only child. A few days later, she arrived at the attorney's office for the reading of his will and discovered that his businesses had been either sold or liquidated and all the proceeds had been left to her. Mary was suddenly a very wealthy woman.

If she hadn't met Bill before her father's death, Mary would have been convinced that he only married her for her money, but Bill was already a wealthy man so he didn't need her inheritance. The truth was Bill was one of her father's business partners and their marriage had been partially arranged. Although Mary's father was emotionally distant, he still wanted to make sure that she was taken care of so he encouraged their "summer-winter" relationship. Bill was closer to her father's age than he was to Mary's so their marriage was cordial, even kind, but it was never loving like you would hope a marriage would be. They were wonderful companions but that was the extent of their relationship.

As they walked through the house, Mary could feel herself getting light-headed. Along with the depression she battled daily, Mary had also developed a set of increasingly troublesome symptoms that not one doctor could explain. Dizziness, shortness of breath, muscle pain so severe it would bring her to her knees, stomach issues, and headaches were just a few of the indicators that something was very wrong. She swayed a little to left and leaned slightly into Bill's shoulder. He looked at her with the same concern and asked if she needed to sit down for a moment. She agreed and sank slowly into a plush armchair that had been left behind by the previous owners. Mary took slow deliberate breaths to help slow down her rapidly beating heart and closed her eyes. "Breathe in," she said to herself, "breathe out. Breathe in," she took a deep breath, "breathe out" and exhaled slowly. Mary repeated this over and over until she could feel her heart rate settle down.

When she opened her eyes again she realized that the sunlight that had once been streaming through the window to her right was starting to dim and she was alone in the room. She pulled her phone out of her purse and checked the time.
5:00pm
Mary had been sitting in that chair for over an hour.

She made one more mental check before she stood up from the chair and realized she was no longer lightheaded so she went in search of the relator and Bill. Both were sitting on the front porch making small talk.

"I am so sorry you two," she stammered apologetically. "I don't know what happened! Bill, why did you let me stay in that chair so long." Bill looked at her and smiled slightly.

"You were sleeping so quietly I didn't have the heart to wake you. That was the most peaceful rest I've seen you get in months." Mary smiled back at her husband and responded.

"Thank you. I haven't been sleeping very well at night have I?" Immediately, Mary began to panic. Bill saw the look of fear on her face and took her hand.

"You didn't say anything in your sleep," he reassured her quietly. One of the other challenges Mary faced, aside from persistent restlessness and night terrors, was she talked in her sleep. Sometimes, they were full-fledged conversations and other times they were angry rants but both were in a language Bill didn't understand. Mary let out a sigh of relief and then perked up.

"Well, if I slept that well in an armchair in this house, imagine the kind of sleep I'll get in a bed! Bill, let's get the house!"

Mary took another long sip of her tea as she continued to stare out into the yard. "Bill never liked that tree" she thought as she smiled softly at the memory. But he didn't get to dislike it long. A little less than a year after they moved in, Bill had a heart attack and died. He had no family and they had no children so it was just Mary in the house alone. She often thought of selling the house and moving into something smaller, and probably would have had she been able to figure out how to take the tree with her. Honestly, Mary could move wherever she wanted. Like her father before him, when Bill died he left all of his money to her so relocating would've been easy but there was something about that tree. She just couldn't bear to leave it.

Mary took the final sip of tea and walked back into the house. It was getting chilly so she decided it was the perfect time to light the fireplace in the front room. Next to the tree, the fireplace was her favorite thing about the house. There was just something about listening to the snap and crackle of the logs being consumed by the fire that brought her some peace.

As she started the fire in the front room, she felt an intense dread envelope her. It came, as it often did, out of the blue. She thought about taking one of the half-dozen medicines she had in the bathroom. In an attempt to minimize her symptoms, the doctors had prescribed no fewer than five different types of narcotics, each of which had a side effect that negatively impacted the others. Taking them was worse than just dealing with symptoms.

"Maybe I'll just take one," she thought as she settled on the sofa with her blanket. "Or maybe…"

Mary got up from the sofa and went over to the large mahogany cabinet positioned to the right of the fireplace by the window. The same window she saw when she woke up in the armchair the day they decided to buy the house. She opened the doors and looked at the many glass decanters, half-full of various brown liquors. On the shelf below, there were bottles of wine and clear liquors, and on the shelf above were the glasses. Mary stood in front of the shelves trying to decide which bottle to pour.

If the tree and the fireplace were Mary's favorite parts of the house, the liquor cabinet was Bill's least favorite. As her symptoms increased and her depression worsened, Bill would often come home to find Mary passed out somewhere in the house, a glass of whatever she'd been drinking knocked over on a counter or spilled on the floor. Eventually, he'd put a lock on the cabinet doors that could only be opened with a key. Mary and Bill didn't argue often, but when they did it was usually as a result of her drinking. It was the way she coped. While she tried to put on a brave face, the truth was that Mary was constantly weighed down by a sense of hopelessness and a fear she couldn't control. The physical issues were one thing. The emotional ones were something entirely different.

Mary often thought that the emotional pain she felt would disappear if the doctors could just find a cure for whatever was wrong with her, but the best they could do was address the symptoms. They could never get to the root of the problem. Nothing on this side of heaven could, Mary decided, so she chose to numb the pain since she couldn't get rid of it. Breaking the lock off the cabinet was one of the first things Mary did after Bill died.

She decided on an unopened bottle of Moscato she'd picked up from her last trip to Italy and looked for the corkscrew. She grabbed a large wine glass from the top shelf in the cabinet and filled it almost to the brim. Instead of putting the cork back in the bottle and placing it back on the bottom shelf, she brought it over to the sofa and set it on the floor. She sat down and took a long pull from her glass. And then another. Her glass was quickly empty so she grabbed the bottle and poured another full glass. It wasn't long until the bottle was empty and Mary found herself back at the cabinet uncorking another one.

This was a familiar scene for her. When the dread and anxiety took over, she could no longer function. She could no longer remember any good days in her life. To her disordered mind, everything had always been this way. She'd always been depressed, always been suicidal, always anxious, always unhappy. Although some part of her knew this wasn't true, there **were** happier times, but in these moments she couldn't remember any of them. The memories always seemed to belong to someone else.

Mary emptied the second bottle and felt herself fall over on the sofa. When she regained consciousness, the first thing she noticed was a pounding headache. The second thing were the voices. Mary never mentioned them to anybody, not even the doctors, for fear of being told she was crazy. The only person who knew she heard them was Bill and that's only because she talked I her sleep. Had she been able to keep her reality to herself, she would have.

"Good job! You've screwed up yet again. Honestly, your whole life consists of a series of screw-ups. That's why you're alone. That's why your mother died, and your father died, and Bill died. No one could stand to be around you. What's wrong with you?!"

Scalding tears singeing her face as each hurled word hit it's mark with shame filled accuracy. She listened quietly as the angry words battered her defeated body. Her latest binge had proven to be much worse than she'd anticipated. Had she really drunk that much?

"You know what? This is just what I expect from someone like you. Congratulations! Two entire bottles! Next time you need to go for three. All you're doing is taking up space in this house, and on this planet. What use are you? I mean, you've always been mediocre, above average at best, but look at yourself. Look!"

"STOP IT!" Mary's anguished scream startled even her. "Leave me alone. Go away...please."

She enveloped her head in her arms and folded herself into a tight little ball. Like a child huddled in a corner, she attempted to fend off the vicious attack, but the words kept coming, full of bile and hatred. They were created to do serious damage.

"You bring nothing but destruction to the lives of the people around you. THAT'S why you're always alone. That's why no one wants you. That's why you've been abandoned."

"I know," Mary said quietly.

She had gotten used to the feelings of loneliness and despair that sheltered her days, her nights. They were so familiar to her that she wondered if she clung to them like some sort of perverted security blanket. They were what she knew and they were consistent, steady, always there no matter how many drinks she had. They ate away at her like maggots devouring decaying flesh, but there was a difference.

Maggots eat dead things. She was being eaten alive, from the inside out.

"You're such a disappointment. Why are you even HERE? You know what you need to do, right?"

Mary unfolded herself and sat up straight. Yes. She knew what she needed to do.

Stumbling as she walked, Mary made her way to the bathroom down the hall.. There, behind the mirror above the sink, was everything she needed. She looked at herself for the first time since the tirade began. Her eyes were rimmed in red and cast black shadows underneath. Whatever light had been was gone and nothing resembling life was left. She looked again.

"This will be easy," Mary thought. She took one of the bottles out of the cabinet and sat on the toilet. She opened the bottle and poured the contents into her lap. They were the most brilliant shade of blue, like little miniature sapphires.

"You know, nobody is even going to miss you, right?"

She started counting 1..2..3..4..5 and figured she could comfortably swallow 10 of the little gems at a time. That would make three handfuls.

"Hmm, let's make it 15," she thought, "Two quick handfuls then, instead of three."

"No one is even going to know that you're gone..."

She grasped the glass that had been placed on the sink next to her. It was cool. She turned on the faucet and filled the glass half-way. Mary took a sip. The water was room temperature. Nope, this wouldn't be difficult at all.

"Well, congratulations. You've proven once again what a failure you are. I hope you can at least get this right."

Taking a deep breath, she shoved the first handful in her mouth followed by a large gulp of water.

"See, easy."

Mary stood up and looked in the mirror again. Who was this woman? The second handful went down as smoothly as the first. She set the glass on the sink. She could feel the nearly three-dozen pills start to dissolve in her stomach, poised and ready to enter her bloodstream. Her eyes were fixated on the swaying figure in the mirror. It was crying, no wait, screaming. She couldn't really tell. Her vision had started to dim and she couldn't hear anything except the beating of her own heart.

Thump Thump. Thump Thump.

How helpless it looked. She wondered if it would be okay.

Thump Thump. Thump Thump.

For the first time in years, she noticed that the persistent, nagging pain was gone.

Thump Thump.

"Thank God," she whispered, eyes closing as she slumped to the floor.

****

Mary's head hurt. The room was spinning and she wasn't quite sure where she was. She was completely unaware of a date and time, but one thing was abundantly clear. She was alive; and someone wasn't happy about it.

"Okay, you? You have to be the biggest failure ever! I mean, seriously. You can't even kill yourself right. What kind of loser can't even commit suicide?!"

"I have no idea," Mary heard herself say in a semi-audible voice. "I have no idea."

As she began to get her bearings, she realized she didn't know if it was morning or evening. And the more she looked around, the more the voices spoke.

"What you need to do is go and try this again. You're still the same woman, with the same problems, the same issues. You're completely and utterly worthless. So, let's try and get this right this time, shall we?"

Mary found herself on the cold tiled floor in the bathroom. She struggled to get up on to her elbows so she could get a better look at her surroundings but she felt like she used to when she was little and would spin around until she got dizzy and fell down.

"I-I can't. I'm too dizzy to stand up and besides I don't have any more pills. I took all thirty the last time."

"Well I guess you'll just have to go to another cabinet and get some more."

Mary could feel the tears growing thick in her chest.

"I-I can't get up. What day is it?! This wasn't the plan! I'm not supposed to be here!"

Nearly instantaneously, confusion turned into panic. Panic, in turn, gave birth to fear.

"I can't think. I don't want to think. God, I don't want to be here! Why am I still here?"

The room was still and she was aware that while she was screaming, it was all in her head. She never actually made a sound.

Still sitting on the floor, Mary could only imagine what her face must have looked like. Eyes, blood shot and red rimmed; the aftereffects of taking 30 extra-strength sleeping pills and waking suddenly to a brand-new day she didn't want to see. Tears spilling forth like torrents of rain soaking the shirt she wore, she held her head and rocked like a child.

"What am I going to do? What am I going to do?"

Out of the tornado that was threatening to tear her apart, came a still small voice. A barely recognizable sound that came from a place Mary was certain had already died.

If what was tormenting you was something that man could fix, he would've fixed it. Your ailment is not of a physical nature, but of a spiritual one and I'm the only one who can fix that.

Mary knew **this** voice, although she hadn't heard it in a while. Not only was it different than the other voices, but it was familiar, comforting. It didn't yell or accuse her. It didn't point the finger and tell her she was a worthless failure. It didn't remind her of everything she'd ever done wrong in her life.

"So, you mean to tell me you can fix all of this? That you have all the answers?"

Yes, and yes.

Mary questioned the voice. "**YOU** can fix me?"

Yes. If you'll let Me.

She thought for a moment. Incredulously, she continued. "Seriously. Not one doctor can figure out how to heal me but you can?"

Yes. If you'll let Me.

"But I'm not worth it. I'm a failure. Didn't you hear what he said?"

Yes. I heard every word

"But I don't have a reason to be here. No one will even miss me. I really don't have a purpose on this Earth."

You may not see your purpose but I do…

And this is where Mary clearly and audibly spoke the words that would forever change her life.

"Okay Lord. I'm giving you one more chance to prove to me that I have a purpose; that I am useful and that I have a reason for being here. That's it Lord. You only get ONE more chance and then I'm calling it quits for real!"

Mary was certain she heard a laugh, an audible chuckle that rumbled deep and low.

Okay. We have a deal.

Suddenly, Mary felt a change. Her body no longer hurt. Her head was no longer spinning and she didn't feel sick. But most of all, the voices were no longer there. She sat on the floor for a moment longer, searching her mind. Were they really gone?

Mary lifted herself up from the floor and looked at herself in the mirror. There was a glow radiating from her face. The face that was staring back at her was not the same one that stared back at her the night before. This face exuded peace and it wasn't a face she'd ever seen before.

As she walked out of the bathroom, she noticed that her entire house was flooded with sunlight. It poured in from every window and blanketed the floor. Had she been a cat, she'd have found a spot on the floor and stretched out in it's warmth. Mary went back to the front room and saw the empty bottles still laying on the floor. She picked them up and shook her head.

"I can't believe you drank all this," she said to herself. It was at that moment that she realized she no longer had a desire to drink. Mary chuckled as she carried the bottles to the recycling bin by the door.

"Never thought I'd see **this** day."

She opened the door and stepped outside on the porch. It was cool and the air was rustling the remaining leaves in the old oak again. She took a deep breath, inhaling the crisp Autumn air. Fall was upon her but on the inside, she felt like Spring. There was a newness of life enveloping her and she could feel it coursing through her body.

Mary wrapped her arms around herself and leaned gently on the rail by the stairs. She stared at the tree and smiled. It seemed to her that the wind increased slightly in response, as if the tree were saying "hello."

Before Mary turned to go back into the house, she looked at the blue sky above the tree.

"Thank you. God, I thank you."

As she walked through the door, she caught herself humming.

Birds flying high, you know how I feel

Sun in the sky, you know how I feel

Reeds driftin' on by you know how I feel

It's a new dawn

It's a new day

It's a new life

For me

And I'm feeling good.

The SHOES Playlist

Ever notice how a good playlist makes any trip better? Whether it's a road trip cross country or your morning or evening commute, good music makes the time spent travelling that much better. On this journey we call life, sometimes we need a playlist to help us just through to the next day. When I was in the hospital, "Waymaker" by Sinach and "There Will Be Glory After This" by JJ Hairston & Youthful Praise gave me hope and encouragement.

As I was finishing this book, I God gave me the idea to come up with a playlist to accompany this book so I began thinking of the songs I listen to when I need to position myself to tackle whatever is coming my way next. And while I know a lot of songs, I needed more. So, what did I do? I reached out to my Facebook Family and asked them to choose one of the categories in this book and give me their favorite Gospel or Contemporary Christian Song. Some songs I'd never heard of and others were songs I hadn't heard in a long time. And while it is by no means a comprehensive list, it does provide quite a few options for you to choose from.

To locate the songs, all you need to do is type the title into Google and enjoy! Or, if you have a music streaming app like Spotify or Apple Music, you can locate them there, download the songs, and create the playlist on your phone.

Whichever way you decide to do it, just know that this list was curated just for you as you take your own journey through Strength, Hope, Overcoming Obstacles, Encouragement, and Success. Enjoy!

STRENGTH

Here I Am: Marvin Sapp
Never Would Have Made It: Le'Andria Johnson
Can't Live: Genita Pugh
Fragile Heart: Yolanda Adams
I Never Lost My Praise: Tremaine Hawkins
Break Every Chain: Tasha Cobbs Leonard
My Soul Has Been Anchored: Douglas Miller
Lord Don't Move My Mountain: Inez Andrews
Order My Steps: GMWA Women of Worship
You Are My Strength: William Murphy
Strength: John P. Kee
Total Praise: Richard Smallwood

HOPE

Yes: Shekinah Glory
Soul's Anthem: Tori Kelly
Exodus: Donald Lawrence and Le'Andria Johnson
Amazing Grace: Kathy Taylor Brown
Optimistic: Sounds of Blackness
Hope Saved My Life: Brian Courtney Wilson
Turning Around for Me: Vashawn Mitchell
All I Need: Brian Courtney Wilson
Psalm 23 (I Am Not Alone): People and Songs
That's When You Blessed Me: LA Mass Choir
The Best Is Yet to Come: Donald Lawrence

You're Next in Line: Shirley Caesar
Imagine Me: Kirk Franklin
Hold On (Change Is Comin'): Sounds of Blackness
Intentional: Travis Greene

OVERCOMING

Speak the Name: Koryn Hawthorne
Psalm 23: The Brooklyn Tabernacle Choir
Declaration: Kirk Franklin
I'll Make Room For You: Jonathan McReynolds
We Fall Down: Donnie McClurkin
Thank You Lord: Walter Hawkins
Lord You Are Good: Todd Galbreth
Let Your Power Fall: Zacardi Cortez
Okay: Kirk Franklin
Immediately: Tasha Cobbs Leonard
My Life is In Your Hands: Kirk Franklin
Alabaster Box: CeCe Winans
My Life, My Love, My All: Kirk Franklin
I Almost Let Go: Kurt Carr
Holy One: Tremaine Hawkins
Let Go: DeWayne Woods

ENCOURAGEMENT

Encourage Yourself: Donald Lawrence and The Tri-City Singers
Better Days: Le'Andria Johnson
Jesus on the Main Line: Ry Cooder
Cry On: Commissioned
No Weapon: Fred Hammond
I Know the Lord Will Make a Way: Smokie Norful
I'm Not Tired Yet: Mississippi Mass Choir
I Believe: James Fortune

You Say: Lauren Diagle
Be Blessed: Yolanda Adams
Be Encouraged: John P Kee
Blessed and Highly Favored: The Clark Sisters
You're Bigger: Jekalyn Carr
Your Destiny: Kevin LaVar
You Know My Name: Tasha Cobbs Leonard
I Won't Go Back: William McDowell

SUCCESS

123 Victory: Kirk Franklin
You Brought the Sunshine: The Clark Sisters
My Testimony: Marvin Sapp
Unstoppable: Koryn Hawthorne
Get Ready for Overflow: Tasha Cobbs Leonard
Well Done: Deitrick Haddon
The Storm is Over Now: Kirk Franklin
Grateful: Hezekiah Walker
You've Been So Faithful: Eddie James
You Made A Way: Travis Greene
Grateful: Hezekiah Walker
Victory: Tye Tribbett
Thank You: Richard Smallwood
You Will Win: Jekalyn Carr
In the Midst of It All: Yolanda Adams

The Marathon Continues

September 4, 2019 was the date of the PT session that ended Chapter 5. So, what's been going on since then? Glad you asked!

- Well, first off, I moved from the short parallel bars to the exercise room where there is one long bar. I was standing with one hand!
- Then, Marjorie, decided to see how I faired using a walker. Wanna guess how I did? (SMILE)
- At my next PT session, I get to try walking with ancillary, or arm, crutches. Take that people who said it wouldn't happen!
- Next up, I'll learn how to use my walker and crutches on a variety of terrains, learn how to get in and out of the car with prostheses on, and whatever else Marjorie decides she thinks I can do. She's been pretty accurate so far!
- I'm going back to see Derek so I can get my legs adjusted. My right leg is longer than my left and I'm too tall for my daughter. Yes. Your read that correctly. I'm too tall for my daughter. She took great pride in being an entire inch taller than me. Now, I'm at least two inches taller than her. That's too tall. I like being 4'11.5". And she likes it too.
- At some point, as I continue to heal, I'll learn how to walk up and down stairs and eventually, I'm determined to run again. I'll let you know how that goes!

Now, since January 1…

- One of my BVCs asked me to come and speak to the teachers at her school. I've been three times already and I am scheduled to return again this school year.
- I presented at my first national education conference since my heart attack and amputations. The ASCD Conference was held in Chicago, IL and my session was completely full. It was awesome!
- I've spoken at a number of churches and I was the baccalaureate speaker at the high school where I used to teach. My former students, colleagues, and parents have been amazingly supportive. One of the reasons why I will always be a Westlake Lion!
- I connected with my favorite photographer and gave myself a photoshoot. Karen Marie Jenkins of Karen Marie Images did my first brand photoshoot years ago and was excited when I contacted her to ask if she would be willing to do another one. Not only did she say yes, she drove all the way from Cincinnati back down to Atlanta to do. Many of my pictures have gone viral and I've been stopped by more than stranger to tell me they've seen them. I am no referred to as "The Lady in the Red Tutu. If you're interested in seeing her work or booking a shoot with her, she can be reached at http://www.karenmarieimages.com/

- Along with my rebranding photos, I needed a new logo. So, after getting the same recommendation from 6 or 7 different people, I began working with AuthenticDNA and its owner Dwight Stellmacher and all I can say is he is anointed to do what he does. Before he designed my logo, he designed the cover for this book and without getting any guidance from me, he created what you see today. Why is this significant? You see the red Chuck Taylor's on the cover? Before my amputations, I was known for wearing my red Chucks to work. It was my signature piece of attire. I didn't tell him that until **after** he showed be the cover. When I asked him how he knew, he said he asked God and that's what He told him. Looking for an amazing graphic designer? Check out my friend Dwight at https://www.authenticdnaapparel.com/
- I was featured in two local magazine articles and have been interviewed on a host of podcasts.
- I was named a *Who's Who in Black Atlanta* for the second year in a row!
- I did my first TEDx Talk! As of the publishing date of this book, the video hasn't been released yet but if you follow me on Facebook or Instagram, I'll let you know when it becomes available. Or, you can just go to my website at www.drchantrise.com and stay abreast of everything I have going on!
- Speaking of how we can stay in touch… Aside from my website, you can follow me on the following platforms:

- Twitter: @DrChantrise
- Instagram: @DrChantrise
- Facebook: Personal Page: Chantrise Holliman
  Business Page: Dr. Chantrise Sims Holliman
- LinkedIn: Chantrise Sims Holliman, EdD.
- Email: Chantrise@DrChantrise.com

Walk in Your Purpose Whether You Have Legs Or Not.

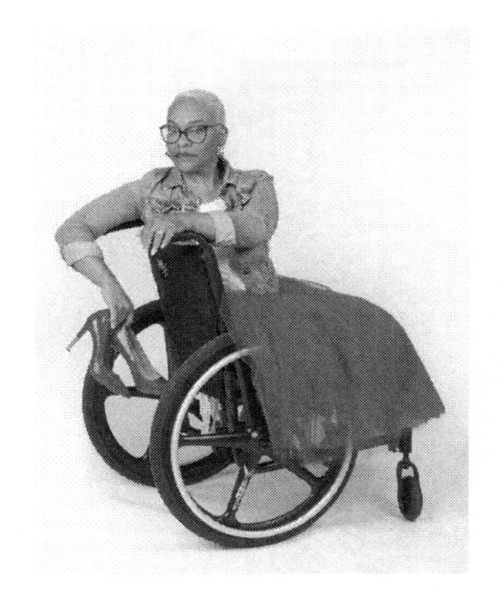

Dr. Chantrise

Made in the USA
Lexington, KY
24 October 2019